SALUTING THE BLOOD OF HEROES

SALUTING THE BLOOD OF HEROES

Behind The Apocalyptic Film

Danny Stewart

BearManor Media

2024

Published in the USA by
BearManor Media
1317 Edgewater Dr. #110
Orlando, FL 32804
www.BearManorMedia.com

Typesetting and layout by PKJ Passion Global

Softcover Edition
ISBN: 979-8-88771-526-1

Printed in the United States of America

Contents

Acknowledgments

I would like to acknowledge all the visionaries who have contributed to the Apocalyptic and post-apocalyptic fiction subgenre. This includes works from both before and after the 1900s, as well as the ongoing dystopian stories that reflect and anticipate the times we live in.

I express my deep appreciation to David and Janet Peoples for consistently engaging in meaningful conversations. I also extend my gratitude to Dennis Maguire, the first assistant director of the epic post-apocalyptic adventure film "The Postman" (1997) for his outstanding work. I have thoroughly enjoyed every discussion with these individuals.

I want to express my thanks to the guest essayists John Kenneth Muir, John Hansen, and Eion Friel for their valuable insights. I truly admire these exceptional individuals who dedicate their passion and effort to the creative process, and I salute them as heroes.

Author Introduction

With this book, I wanted to explore the history and popularity of apocalyptic and post-apocalyptic fiction in literature and media. These stories tap into our fears and anxieties of the unknown, making them fascinating to humans. One lesser-known film in this subgenre is "The Salute of the Jugger" (released as "The Blood of Heroes" in the United States), directed by David Webb Peoples, a veteran of the genre, in his first and only directing job. I aim to shed light on this film and its place in the subgenre of science fiction sports movies such as "Rollerball," "Futuresport," "Death Race 2000," "The Running Man," and "Battle Royale." David Eggby, the director of photography on the original "Mad Max," photographed the film, capturing the dusty, dirty setting and characters with a rawness that perfectly suits the film's atmosphere. The score for the film was crafted by Todd Bokelheide, known for his remarkable work on the documentaries "Hearts of Darkness: A Filmmaker's Apocalypse and Ballets Russes." The soundtrack showcases primal drums and pioneering percussion, resulting in a grand and enigmatic score that perfectly captures the film's primal tone. Guy Norris, a known stuntman, director, and actor, worked on "The Road Warrior" and later "Mad Max: Fury Road." He was a second unit director and stunt coordinator on the film and played a vital role in coordinating the sport of Jugging. Richard Francis-Bruce edited the film and had worked on "Mad Max Beyond Thunderdome." He also worked with director George Miller on "The Witches of Eastwick" and "Lorenzo's Oil." After "Jugger," he went on to receive three Oscar nominations for the films "The Shawshank Redemption," "Se7en," and "Air Force One." His career is nothing less than stellar. In the world of Jugger, Joan Chen's portrayal of Kidda stands out as a powerful force, similar to other notable female characters such as Sigourney Weaver's Ripley in the "Aliens" series and Charlize Theron's Furiosa in "Mad Max Fury Road." Although Rutger Hauer is no longer with us, his portrayal of Sallow, an experienced veteran of the sport, has left a lasting impression. Both Kidda and Sallow drive the narrative forward with captivating and emotionally resonant performances. Together, they lead the pack, showcasing their strength and resilience. Alongside them are fellow cast members Vincent D'Onofrio, Delroy Lindo, Anna Katarina, Justin Monjo, Hugh Keays-Byrne, Max Fairchild, and Gandhi MacIntyre, who also elevate the film.

"The Salute of the Jugger" is not apocalyptic, but rather post-something, deliberately vague about what happened. It's dystopian, where something has gone wrong, and we're back in the Middle Ages. In contrast to "Twelve Monkeys," where the filmmakers decided to use germs instead of nuclear explosions, director and screenwriter David Webb Peoples wanted "The Salute of the Jugger" to be even vaguer, leaving the cause of the world's decline up to interpretation. The film's intention was not to follow clichés but to create a unique and mysterious world. One of the taglines for the film states, "The time will come when winning is everything," reflecting the primal, violent game at the center of the story.

Since its release, "The Salute of the Jugger" has gained a dedicated fanbase and achieved cult classic status. This has led to the creation of a new sport called Jugger, inspired by the movie. Jugger follows similar rules to the hyper-violent football variation depicted in the film, although without the violence and dog skull. Like the "Mad Max" films that have influenced global culture, "The Salute of the Jugger" explores themes of resilience, rivalry, and human perseverance in a harsh and isolated environment. Despite not receiving widespread recognition or financial success, the film's distinct setting, raw atmosphere, and intense portrayal of the sport have contributed to its growing popularity among its loyal fanbase. I wanted to convey the blood, sweat, and tears that go into the genre of these stories while also conveying the emotion and hard work that goes into the filmmaking process.

Author Danny Stewart spent much of his time on top of Reigate Hill in the United Kingdom during the Covid-19 pandemic. He found the location to be an ideal space for reflection, peace, tranquillity, and breathtaking scenery that fostered ideas for writing and an escape from the horrors of the world that humanity was experiencing, which felt like one of the many post-apocalyptic tales written in fiction or portrayed in film.

Apocalyptic and post-apocalyptic fiction – The Birth of a Sub-Genre

The apocalypse is also depicted in visual art, for example in Albert Goodwin's painting Apocalypse (1903).[1]

Apocalyptic and post-apocalyptic stories found within the science fiction genre depict the downfall or destruction of societies on Earth or other planets. These events can range from catastrophes, viral pandemics, zombie outbreaks and takeovers by artificial intelligence to invasions by extraterrestrial beings, uncontrollable shifts in climate patterns and impacts from celestial bodies. For example, the movie "When Worlds Collide" released in 1951 and based on the 1933 novel by Edwin Balmer and Philip Wylie showcases a scenario where a rogue planet collides, with Earth. Throughout this discussion we will explore authors who have emerged from this genre. Visionary thinkers who have seemingly foreseen potential future disasters.

JOHN W. CAMPBELL, JR.

John W Campbell Jr. c. 1932.
Stellar Publishing / Wonder Stories, January 1932.[2]

John W. Campbell Jr. left an enduring mark on the science fiction genre as both an author and editor. He spent 34 years at the helm of *Astounding Science Fiction* (currently referred to as *Analog Science Fiction* and *Truth*), shaping the publication and the style overall. His influence encompassed the abilities he fostered during the "Golden Age of Sci-fi," leaving an enduring effect on the genre.

Although Campbell was mostly related to hard sci-fi and speculative concepts as opposed to apocalyptic stories, his payment to the genre is indisputable. He wrote many significant items that explored clinical ideas, technological innovations, and social adjustments. One such noteworthy job is the novella "Who Goes There?" The story focuses on a group of researchers stationed in Antarctica who uncover an ancient alien spacecraft hidden deep within the ice. The story introduces a shape-shifting extraterrestrial life that can imitate other living organisms flawlessly. As the scientists attempt to uncover which among them might have been taken over by this mystical alien, stress and fear escalate, resulting in a thrilling and suspenseful story. The novella was adjusted into feature films, including Howard Hawks' and Christian Nyby's "The Thing from Another World" (1951), John Carpenter's "The Thing" (1982), and a prequel to the 1982 movie labelled "The Thing" (2011). "The Thing" became part of what was later described as Carpenter's "Apocalypse Trilogy," which contained three films: "The Thing," "Prince of Darkness," and "In the Mouth of Madness." All three movies had grim endings for their characters. In John Carpenter's later movie "Ghosts of Mars," Braddock (played by Pam Grier) states, "Who goes there?" This is the same title as the original novel. John Carpenter's earlier movie, "Halloween" (1978), also paid homage when the protagonist is shown viewing "The Thing from Another World" on television.

Theatrical poster for the American release of the 1951
film The Thing from Another World.[3]

"Did Hawks direct it? That's one of the most inane and ridiculous questions I've ever heard, and people keep asking. That it was Hawks' style. Of course it was. This is a man I studied and

wanted to be like. You would certainly emulate and copy the master you're sitting under, which I did. Anyway, if you're taking painting lessons from Rembrandt, you don't take the brush out of the master's hands."—Christian Nyby[1]

Film critic Roger Ebert wrote about "The Thing from Another World" in a 1982 review of the Carpenter's "The Thing," stating "The Two 1950's versions ... (The Thing from Another World and Invasion of the Body Snatchers) were seen at the time as fables based on McCarthyism; communists, like victims of The Thing, looked, sounded, and acted like your best friend, but they were infected with a deadly secret."[2]

Film critic Nick Schager wrote on the films' themes, stating "An early remark by one military official concerning the burgeoning Soviet presence in the North Pole reinforces the Thing's allegorical status as communist 'other' (one can deduce that Hendry fears the creature not only because it's emotionless and sexless, but also godless)."[3]

John Carpenter's film "The Thing" from 1982 is heavily influenced by the 1938 novella "Who Goes There?" written by John W. Campbell Jr. This film successfully captures the essence of the original story, creating a masterpiece that is filled with claustrophobic paranoia. Leading the cast is Kurt Russell, who plays the role of R.J. MacReady, the team's helicopter pilot, with notable performances by A. Wilford Brimley, T. K. Carter, David Clennon, Keith David, Richard Dysart, Charles Hallahan, Peter Maloney, Richard Masur, Donald Moffat, Joel Polis, and Thomas G. Waites in supporting roles. Despite

---

[1] *Henry Fuhrmann "A 'Thing' to His Credit." Los Angeles Times, May 25, 1997.*

[2] *Smith, Jeff (2014). Film Criticism, the Cold War, and the Blacklist: Reading the Hollywood Reds. Berkeley, California: University of California Press. p. 9. ISBN 978-0-520-28068-7. Similarly, once critics identified Invasion of the Body Snatchers as a film expressing an underlying tension about the threat of communism, others found similar patterns in The Thing [from Another World] (1951).*

[3] *Nick Schager (August 13, 2003). "Review: The Thing from Another World." Slant Magazine.*

initially receiving negative reviews in 1982, "The Thing" faced tough competition from Steven Spielberg's optimistic alien film, "E.T. the Extra-Terrestrial." This, combined with the saturated market of successful science fiction and fantasy movies during the summer of 1982, made it challenging for "The Thing" to resonate with audiences experiencing a recession. The film's nihilistic and bleak tone clashed with the prevailing sentiment at the time. Likewise, "Blade Runner" faced a similar fate, being released during the time of "E.T.," but both films have since gained recognition as cinematic classics. Filmmakers have noted its influence on their work, particularly Quentin Tarantino. During an interview with Stephen Colbert, he said, "I love Howard Hawks' The Thing and I love John Carpenter's The Thing... Rob Bottin's effects in that movie are some of the greatest practical special effects ever put on a movie theater screen."[4]

The movies "Reservoir Dogs" and "The Hateful Eight" directed by Tarantino were heavily influenced by "The Thing" in their depiction of paranoia. Additionally, "The Hateful Eight," featuring Kurt Russell, takes place in a lodge during a snowstorm, in Wyoming. The renowned Italian composer Ennio Morricone created the score for John Carpenters "The Thing." Morricone's extraordinary musical talent also led him to compose the score for "The Hateful Eight" in 2015 earning him the esteemed Academy Award, for Best Original Score. Several notable filmmakers, such as Guillermo del Toro,[5] James DeMonaco,[6] J.J. Abrams,[7] Neill Blomkamp,[8] David

---

[4] *The Late Show with Stephen Colbert https://youtu.be/Wv0BrPtiDRk?si=tuy3pvx-t7O46aMps*

[5] *Michael Nordine (May 23, 2016). "Guillermo del Toro Praises John Carpenter in Epic Twitter Marathon." IndieWire.*

[6] *Ryan Lambie (February 17, 2016). "John Carpenter: analysing his style and growing influence." Den of Geek.*

[7] *Geoff Boucher (April 22, 2011). "J.J. Abrams: Seven films that shaped 'Super 8'." Pitchfork.*

[8] *Andrew Liptak (July 12, 2017). "Neill Blomkamp on creating the horrific creature in his latest short film Zygote." The Verge.*

Robert Mitchell,[9] Rob Hardy,[10] Steven S. DeKnight,[11] John Sayles, and Edgar Wright, have expressed their admiration for "The Thing" or acknowledged its impact on their own projects.[12] Since its initial release, "The Thing" has undergone a substantial reassessment among both critics and fans, now widely acknowledged as a significant benchmark and a true masterpiece in the genres of paranoia and practical effects. *Empire* magazine selected it as one of "The 500 Greatest Movies of All Time."[13] The following publications have also recognized it as one of the best films of 1982, including Filmsite.org, Film.com, and *Entertainment Weekly*.

On the left is the author Danny Stewart and on the right is John Carpenter in June 2016.

---

[9] Drew Taylor (March 12, 2015). *"Director David Robert Mitchell Reveals The 5 Biggest Influences On 'It Follows'." IndieWire.*

[10] Jim Hemphill (2015). *"The Thing." American Cinematographer.*

[11] Scott Meslow (March 23, 2018). *"Steven DeKnight Went From Pacific Rim Fanboy to Pacific Rim Uprising Director." GQ.*

[12] Jason Zinoman (August 19, 2011). *"What Spooks the Masters of Horror?." The New York Times.*

[13] *"Empire's The 500 Greatest Movies of All Time." Empire. (2008).*

**"It's better to be a human being than an imitation,
or let ourselves be taken over by this creature
who's not necessarily evil, but whose nature it is to simply
imitate, like a chameleon."—John Carpenter[14]**

Film critic Sarah Boslaugh stated in her review that the film ."stays truer to its source material, John W. Campbell, Jr.'s 1938 novella Who Goes There?, than the 1951 Howard Hawks-Christian Nyby feature The Thing from Another World."[15]

James O'Ehley of Sci-Fi Movie Page commentated, "The ending is suitably downbeat, and John Carpenter makes effective use of his source material - there is a real sense of paranoia (after all, the alien could be any of the men at the research station) and real tension hanging over the onscreen proceedings."[16]

Steve Biodrowski of ESplatter wrote, "Carpenter's rethinking of producer Howard Hawks' classic is an honorable attempt to hew closer to the original story."[17]

Rob Vaux, from Flipside Movie Emporium, described "The Thing" in his review as, "A work of pure suspense unseen since the days of Hitchcock, expertly blended with some of the most gruesome effects ever conceived. The Thing is a brilliant horror film by any standard."[18]

---

14 *Jonathan Rosenbaum (July 10, 1982). "On Location with John Carpenter's The Thing." JonathanRosenbaum.net. - https://jonathanrosenbaum.net/2022/10/on-location-with-john-carpenters-the-thing-tk/*

15 *Sarah BoslaughPlayback:stl http://www.playbackstl.com/movie-reviews/11035-halloween-creep-out-three-by-john-carpenter*

16 *James O'EhleySci-Fi Movie Page https://www.scifimoviepage.com/thing.html*

17 *http://cinefantastiqueonline.com/2007/08/26/hollywood-gothique-some-thing-wicked-this-way-comes/*

18 *Rob Vaux Flipside Movie Emporium (January 17, 2003).*

Portrait Still of English film director Alfred Hitchcock (1899–1980).[4]

Alfred Hitchcock, born on August 13 1899 and passed away on April 29 1980 gained recognition as the esteemed "Master of Suspense." Interestingly, he often made cameo appearances in his films and also took up the role of host and producer for the television series "Alfred Hitchcock Presents" from 1955 to 1962 and "The Alfred Hitchcock Hour" from 1962 to 1965. Over the course of his career he received an impressive total of 46 nominations, for Academy Awards and emerged victorious in six categories. It is worth noting that despite being nominated five times for Best Director he unfortunately never managed to secure this sought after accolade.

Hitchcock earned acclaim for his ability to create intense psychological thrillers that captivated audiences. While his films typically centered on crime, and mystery. "The Birds" (1963) was a departure from his usual style as it incorporated a subtle apocalyptic undertone. This film portrayed a string of perplexing bird attacks, on a quaint town highlighting the erosion of norms and the unsettling fear of the inexplicable rather than focusing on the complete destruction of the world.

Theatrical poster for the film The Birds (1963).[5]

"The Birds" derived its inspiration from a real-life incident that took place on August 18, 1961, in Capitola, California, a seaside town. The incident shattered the calm morning as residents of Capitola were faced with a frightening spectacle. Swarms of seabirds, behaving like something out of a horror film, besieged their homes. The chaos caused by the birds colliding with cars and leaving partially digested anchovies scattered across lawns left the residents of Capitola in terror.[19]

In the 1960s, Alfred Hitchcock became aware of this incident and used it as valuable research material for his ongoing film project. At the time, the true cause behind the birds' peculiar behavior was undiscovered, but it was later revealed that toxic algae was responsible for their aggressive actions.[20]

---

[19] *Laurel Hamers (December 7, 2015). "The Hitchcock movie was inspired by crab toxin." The Mercury News.*

[20] *Wynne Parry (January 3, 2012). "Blame Hitchcock's Crazed Birds on Toxic Algae." Live Science.*

Joseph Pennell's 1918 prophetic Liberty bond poster calls up the pictorial image of a bombed New York City, totally engulfed in a firestorm. At the time, the armaments available to the world's various air forces were not powerful enough to produce such a result.[6]

Another potential factor that could lead to an apocalypse is the depletion of vital resources as showcased in the 1979 film "Mad Max" directed by George Miller. This movie portrays a world struggling with energy shortages caused by the exhaustion of oil reserves resulting in a breakdown of law and order. The story revolves around clashes between law enforcement agencies and criminal motorcycle gangs ultimately leading to the collapse of modern society and the outbreak of nuclear warfare as depicted in "Mad Max 2: The Road Warrior" (1981). The introduction of "The Road Warrior" suggests that the scarcity of fuel was a consequence of reaching peak oil production and the destruction of oil reserves during a conflict, in the Middle East. In the aftermath surviving remnants of society manage to scrape by through scavenging or utilizing methane produced from pig waste as illustrated in the film "Mad Max Beyond Thunderdome" (1985). Screenwriter James McCausland drew significant inspiration from his observations of the repercussions of the 1973 oil crisis on Australian drivers.

"George and I wrote the [Mad Max] script based on the thesis that people would do almost anything to keep vehicles moving and the assumption that nations would not consider the huge costs of providing infrastructure for alternative energy until it was too late." —James McCausland, writing on peak oil in *The Courier-Mail*, 2006[21]

"Mad Max is a very dark film. We begin with an admittedly harsh world, but Max is a fairly normal man, working a day job as a highway cop, and having a wife and baby at home…. But the world catches up to him and his family is decimated; and he descends into his dark side. By the end of the film, mad, angry, crazy Max has become a full monster, the avenging demon."—George Miller[22]

In this subgenre, numerous allegories have been explored by both critics and scholars. One example of such a masterpiece is the Australian post-apocalyptic dystopian action film, "Mad Max 2: The Road Warrior." Critic Jeffrey M. Anderson wrote, "Miller has just as much to say about human behavior and industrialization as he does about fast cars."[23] Sean Axmaker Stream on Demand wrote, "Think of it as a spaghetti western on wheels, or a samurai adventure in the ashes of the end of the world, executed with comic book color and punk fashions."[24]

---

[21] *James McCausland (4 December 2006). "Scientists' warnings unheeded." The Courier-Mail. News.com.au.*

[22] *https://thefilmist.wordpress.com/2009/09/19/danny-peary-on-mad-max-2the-road-warrior/*

[23] *Gas Knuckles by Jeffrey M. Anderson https://www.combustiblecelluloid.com/classic/roadwarr.shtml*

[24] *Sean Axmaker Stream on Demand https://streamondemandathome.com/road-warrior-gibson-miller-dvd-blu-ray-vod/*

"Mad Max 2: The Road Warrior" has made a considerable impact on popular culture, surpassing the boundaries of cinema. Esteemed filmmakers, such as Guillermo del Toro, David Fincher, Robert Rodriguez, and Zack Snyder, have expressed their profound admiration for the movie, regarding it as one of their favorites. Hideo Kojima, the director of the critically acclaimed "Metal Gear Solid" video game series, also holds "Mad Max 2" in high esteem. The film's influence even extends to the world of manga, with noted author Buronson drawing inspiration from it for his manga and anime series "Fist of the North Star." Notably, David Twohy, the co-writer of "Waterworld," attributes "Mad Max 2" as a significant influence on his own film, both of which share the same talented cinematographer, Dean Semler.

The third installment of the "Mad Max" franchise, "Mad Max Beyond Thunderdome," has also had a significant impact on popular culture due to its unique elements within the "Mad Max" universe. Notable highlights include Tina Turner's performance as Aunty Entity and her contributions to the film's soundtrack with songs like "We Don't Need Another Hero (Thunderdome)" and "One of the Living." The depiction of Bartertown also stands out, and the film has been recognized as a source of inspiration by filmmaker Chris Weitz.[25] The film draws inspiration from Russell Hoban's novel "Riddley Walker" and William Golding's "Lord of the Flies," which is clearly evident in its themes and ideas.

"Riddley Walker" is a novel published in 1980, authored by Russell Hoban. Hoban drew inspiration for the book from the medieval wall painting of the legend of Saint Eustace at Canterbury Cathedral, and began working on it in 1974. The story is set in a post-apocalyptic world where society has been devastated by a nuclear war and about 2,000 years have passed. The narrative is delivered by the

---

[25]   *Robert Saucedo (1 August 2014). "Meet Chris Weitz, director of ABOUT A BOY and AMERICAN PIE, this weekend at Vintage Park!" Alamo Drafthouse Cinema.*

young protagonist, Riddley Walker, who lives in a primitive society that has emerged from the remnants of the old world.

Saint Eustace the inspiration for Riddley Walker.[7]

Cinematographer Dean Semler discussed the challenges of making the film. "Mad Max Beyond Thunderdome" proved far more challenging than "Mad Max 2." We were dealing with more varied environments than before and it was essential that each of the worlds created for the film have a distinctly different look."[26]

The term "Thunderdome" has since become widely used to describe a high-stakes contest with dire consequences for the losing side.[27] Roger Ebert, a critic from the *Chicago Sun-Times*, said about "Thunderdome" as "the first really original movie idea about how to stage a fight since we got the first karate movies" and "one of the great creative action scenes in the movies."[28]

---

[26] *Phil Edwards (September 1985). "Mad Max: Beyond Thunderdome." American Cinematographer. 66 (9).*

[27] *Henry McCusker (14 October 2013). ""Thunderdome" is a euphemism for a contest where the loser suffers harsh consequences." Regenerative Medicine Investors. Hopkinton, MA: Scimitar Equity.*

[28] *"Mad Max Beyond Thunderdome." Chicago Sun-Times.*

Fans of the series have criticized the film for being lighter in tone than its predecessors. Nick Rogers of *Midwest Film Journal* summed it up in his review, stating that "If "Mad Max" embraced a geneticist's acumen and "The Road Warrior" a philosopher's spirit, "Thunderdome" is about cold, hard economics - not just in Bartertown's transactions but the market expectations that come with the receipt of studio funding."[29]

In a 1985 interview with *Time Out* magazine during the release of "Mad Max Beyond Thunderdome," George Miller stated, "Bartertown had to be a little microcosm of modern day society, so we tried to account for everything [there], you know… the equivalent of the police force, and the military. Tina Turner was kind of a politician and a feudal lord, the Underworld and Master Blaster were a form of the energy, so there was a dialogue going between the people who ruled the place and people who produced things."[30]

"In Japan, they saw it as a samurai film. The French called it a western on wheels. In Scandinavia, it was a Viking movie. And I was smart enough to know that this wasn't as a result of anything I'd done consciously. If the work had gone smoothly I might have fallen victim to hubris."
—George Miller on Mad Max[31]

Director George Miller described "Mad Max: Fury Road" as a "very simple allegory, almost a western on wheels."[32]The fourth installment of the Mad Max series emphasizes three crucial elements:

---

29   *https://midwestfilmjournal.com/2015/04/28/class-of-1985-mad-max-beyond-thunderdome/*

30   *https://multiglom.com/2015/05/12/george-miller-the-1985-interview/*

31   *'We're hardwired for stories': Mad Max director George Miller on myths, medicine and a pointy-eared Idris Elba by Xan Brooks https://www.theguardian.com/film/2022/aug/18/mad-max-director-george-miller-interview-idris-elba*

32   *Ben Child, "Comic-Con 2014: Mad Max: Fury Road roars into view." The Guardian. (28 July 2014).*

blood, oil, and water. The franchise's narrative has been shaped by various literary works and real-world events, drawing inspiration from Joseph Campbell's teachings and incorporating elements of the hero's journey. Joseph Campbell presented his concept in his 1949 publication, "The Hero with a Thousand Faces," which outlines a universal pattern observed in mythical tales and stories from diverse cultures. This pattern follows the hero as they embark on a quest for self-discovery and transformation, progressing through several stages. Max Rockatansky is the protagonist and antihero of the "Mad Max" series, brought to life by director George Miller and producer Byron Kennedy. He was portrayed by Mel Gibson in the first three films released between 1979 and 1985, and later by Tom Hardy in the 2015 fourth installment. Max Rockatansky was ranked 75th on Total Film's prestigious Top 100 Movie Characters of All Time list.[33]

In the above-mentioned scenarios, the post-apocalyptic genre also explores pandemics as a prominent theme. A notable example is the 1954 horror novel titled "I Am Legend" by American author Richard Matheson. Mary Shelley's novel "The Last Man," which revolves around a survivor immune to a devastating plague, greatly influenced Matheson's work. "I Am Legend" has since had a significant impact on zombie and vampire literature, popularizing the concept of a global apocalypse triggered by disease. The novel was later adapted into the films "The Last Man on Earth" (1964), "The Omega Man" (1971), and "I Am Legend" (2007), while also inspiring George A. Romero's iconic "Night of the Living Dead" (1968). Romero discussed the creation of the film:

"I had written a short story, which I basically had ripped off from a Richard Matheson novel called I Am Legend."—George Romero[34]

---

[33] *"The Total Film Top 100 Movie Characters Of All Time - 75 to 51." Total Film. 28 September 2007).*

[34] *"One for the Fire: The Legacy of Night of the Living Dead"—Night of the Living Dead DVD, 2008, Region 1, Dimension Home Entertainment*

Screenshot from the trailer for the film Night of the Living Dead (1968).[8] Walter Reade Organization, Inc. - Night Of The Living Dead (1968) - Trailer

The "Dead" series by George Romero comprises of six horror films that follow different groups struggling to survive during a zombie apocalypse. Numerous critics have analyzed Romero's movies as social critiques. For example, "Night of the Living Dead" is often interpreted as a response to the turbulent events of the 1960s, while "Dawn of the Dead" is regarded as a satirical commentary on consumerism. Similarly, "Day of the Dead" explores the conflict between science and the military, while "Land of the Dead" delves into the complexities of class struggle. "The Living Dead," a horror novel published in 2020, is a result of collaboration between George A. Romero and Daniel Kraus. Tragically, the book remained unfinished after Romero's death in 2017. In honor of Romero's legacy and to fulfill his vision, Kraus was recruited to complete the novel's conclusion.[35]

Author Stephen King[36] said: "Books like I Am Legend were an inspiration to me."

---

[35] *Bill Sheehan (September 2, 2020). "George Romero's posthumous epic, 'The Living Dead,' reads like a definitive account of the zombie apocalypse." The Washington Post.*

[36] *"The Legend that inspired me." The Times. London. 2006-07-22*

"The writer's job is to use the tools in his or her toolbox to get as much of each one out of the ground intact as possible. Sometimes the fossil you uncover is small, a seashell. Sometimes it's enormous, a Tyrannosaurus Rex with all those gigantic ribs and grinning teeth. Either way, short story or thousand-page whopper of a novel, the techniques of excavation remain basically the same."—Stephen King[37]

Tim Cain, the producer, lead programmer, and one of the primary designers of the computer game "Fallout" released in 1997, mentioned that he drew inspiration from the novel "I Am Legend" and the movie "The Omega Man" while developing the game.

"This book was how a[n] individual would handle thinking that he was the last survivor on Earth. This is why in Fallout 1 when you're voted to leave the Vault, we really wanted that sense of isolationism; that sense of: You are the only person out here on the Wasteland who is, quote, 'a normal person', and we wanted you to feel, like, special in that way."[38]

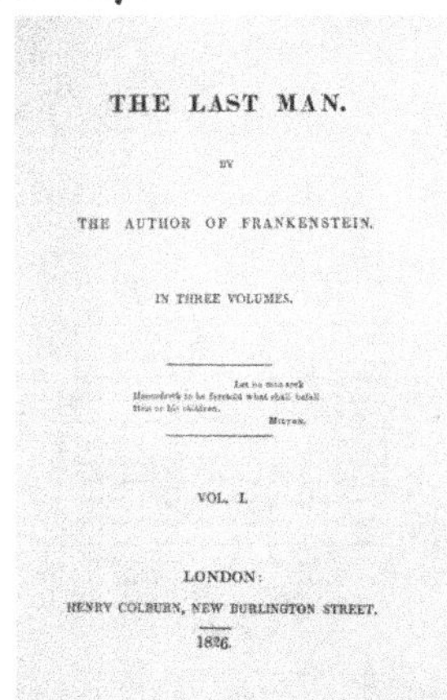

The Last Man 1st ed title pg[9]

---

[37] *Stephen King, (2000). On Writing: A Memoir of the Craft. pp. 163–164.*

[38] *GameSpot (2012-03-09), Fallout Classic Revisited*

Mary Shelley's novel, "The Last Man," holds a notable place in literary history as one of the earliest works of dystopian fiction. Despite its significance, the book initially faced severe criticism and remained relatively obscure upon its publication in 1826. It was only during the 1960s that the novel garnered attention and started gaining wider recognition among readers.

Set in Europe during the late 21st century, "The Last Man" unfolds against the backdrop of a devastating bubonic plague pandemic that emerges and swiftly engulfs the whole world, leading to the near-extinction of humanity. Alongside this central theme, the novel delves into the concept of a British republic, with Shelley herself actively participating in meetings held in the House of Commons to gain insights into the governance system of the Romantic era. Throughout the narrative, Shelley incorporates various fictional references to her late husband, Percy Bysshe Shelley, who tragically died in a shipwreck four years before the book's publication. Additionally, Lord Byron, a close friend of the Shelley's who had passed away two years earlier, is also mentioned in the novel.

Eileen Hunt Botting of the University of Notre Dame has stated that the novel "saw that the disaster of a pandemic would be driven by politics," and that the "spiraling health crisis would be caused by what people and their leaders had done and failed to do on the international stage — in trade, war and the interpersonal bargains, pacts and conflicts that precede them."[39] Botting has further described the novel as identifying [40]"three patterns of modern democratic corruption, which would be exposed and exacerbated by a pandemic:

---

[39]	*Eileen Hunt Botting (13 March 2020). "Mary Shelley Created 'Frankenstein,' and Then a Pandemic". The New York Times.*

[40]	*Eileen Hunt Botting (2021). "Predicting the Patriarchal Politics of Pandemics From Mary Shelley to COVID-19". Frontiers in Sociology. 6. doi:10.3389/ fsoc.2021.624909. ISSN 2297-7775*

1. **slow yet steady institutional erosion of norms and practices of trust and equality;**
2. **authoritarian forms of populism that betray the people who bring an executive leader to power; and**
3. **patriarchal and religious forms of populism that manipulate the people's beliefs through fear and disinformation."**

The novel also tackles the xenophobia displayed by imperial European nations towards other regions of the world. As noted by Olivia Murphy, a scholar at the University of Sydney, the novel demonstrates that "this sense of racial superiority and immunity is unfounded: all people are united in their susceptibility to the fatal disease."[41]

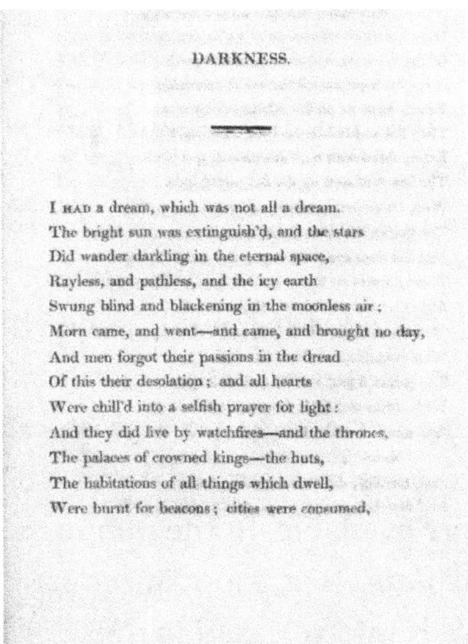

First page from the 1816 collection The Prisoner of Chillon.

Lord Byron wrote the poem "Darkness" in July 1816 as part of the collection called "The Prisoner of Chillon." The poem explores the theme of a catastrophic and apocalyptic end to the world.[10]

---

41   *Olivia Murphy (4 May 2020). "Guide to the Classics: Mary Shelley's The Last Man is a prophecy of life in a global pandemic". The Conversation.*

The Book of Daniel is one of the earliest instances of
apocalyptic literature within the Abrahamic traditions.[11]

H.G. Wells, an extremely prolific English author, is best known for
his literary masterpieces "The War of the Worlds" (1898) , "The
Time Machine" (1895), "The Invisible Man" (1897), "The Island of
Doctor Moreau" (1896), and "The First Men in the Moon" (1901).

H.G. Wells also created stories and essays that explored various
subjects beyond the confines of science fiction. It is undeniable that
Wells had an influence on the genre and literature in general. On
August 13 1946 H.G. Wells departed from this world. Nowadays
many of his works are available, in the public domain.

"The Time Machine" is a captivating science fiction novella
penned by H. G. Wells and released in 1895. It has gained acclaim
for its role in popularizing the notion of time travel. Within the
story Wells presents the concept of utilizing a vehicle or device
to purposefully traverse through moments in time which we now
commonly refer to as a "time machine."[42]

---

[42] *Pilkington, Ace G. (2017). Science Fiction and Futurism: Their Terms and Ideas.
McFarland. p. 137.*

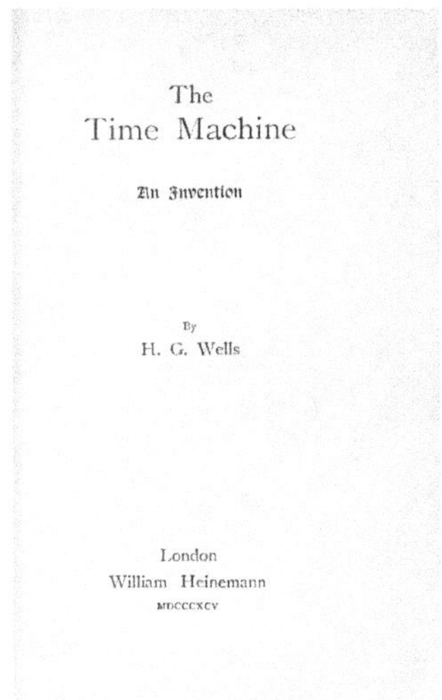

Title page of the original edition of The Time Machine.[12] - Herbert George Wells - The Time Machine (H. G. Wells, William Heinemann, 1895)

The Time Machine was reprinted in Two Complete Science-Adventure Books in 1951.[13] - Wings Publishing / Allen Anderson

H. G. Wells as depicted in Gernsback's Science Wonder Stories in 1929.[14]

H. G. Wells pioneering novel, "The War of the Worlds," transformed the world of science fiction by introducing the notion of extraterrestrial invasion, which has since become a significant subgenre within the larger genre. These tales showcase aliens from other worlds making their way onto Earth, conquering and dominating.

Ever since its publication, "The War of the Worlds" has been the source of inspiration for numerous adaptations in various forms of media. To date, there have been seven films, radio dramas, comic books, video games, television shows, as well as sequels or parallel stories written by other authors. Many of these adaptations happen in diverse locations or time periods, not taking place in the same setting as the original novel.

One notable adaptation is the 1938 radio broadcast narrated and directed by Orson Welles. In this broadcast, the first two-thirds of the 60-minute program were presented as news bulletins, creating a sense of realism. This caused widespread outrage and panic among listeners who believed the events described in the program to be real.[43]

---

[43]   *Alan Brinkley, (2010). "Chapter 23 – The Great Depression." The Unfinished Nation. McGraw-Hill Education. p. 615. ISBN 978-0-07-338552-5.*

First edition cover of the novel "The War of the Worlds" by H. G. Wells. The image is in public domain because the author died more than 70 years ago.[15]

Title page, 1927 Amazing Stories reprint, cover illustration by Frank R. Paul.[16]Amazing Stories® is a Registered Trademark of The Experimenter Publishing Company, LLC.https://amazingstories.com/

Alien tripod illustration by Alvim Corréa, from the 1906 French edition of H.G. Wells' "War of the Worlds."[17] Henrique Alvim Corrêa - Wells, H.G. War of the Worlds (1906, French ed.)

Illustration for a 1906 edition of H. G. Wells's 1898 The War of the Worlds.[18]

Martian Emerges, from The War of the Worlds, Belgium edition, 1906 Pencil and ink on paperboard 13.125 x 10.25 in. (sheet) Not signed The War of the Worlds Archive This illustration is featured in Book I: The Coming of the Martians, Chapter IV: "The Cylinder Opens," 1906.

The Sleeper Awakes[19]

The novel "The Sleeper Awakes" by H. G. Wells explores a dystopian world where a man falls into a deep sleep that lasts for over two centuries. When he finally wakes up, he discovers that London has completely transformed, with society having undergone significant changes. Shockingly, he realizes that he has become the richest person on Earth without his knowledge. As he adjusts to a reality that surpasses even his wildest imagination, he is suddenly confronted with the disturbing and terrifying aspects of this futuristic society. The plot of Woody Allen's 1973 film "Sleeper" bears resemblance to certain aspects of the storyline in the novel.[44]

Floyd C. Gale of Galaxy Science Fiction said of The Sleeper Awakes: "impossibly timid" and outdated science, "The worth of the story lies in its human values… This is 'Young Wells' at his non-Utopian best."[45]

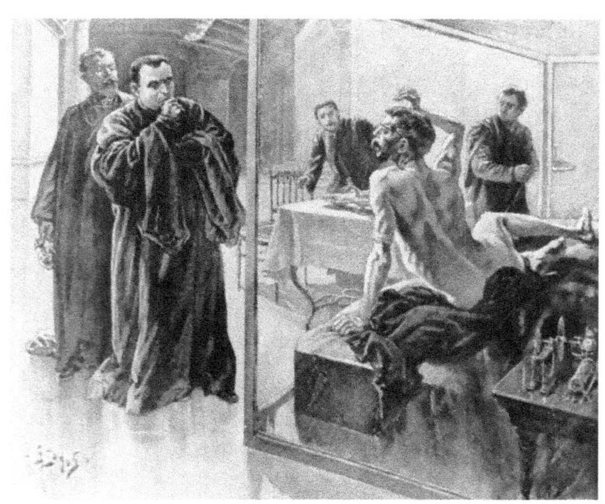

"Graham awakens unexpectedly." Art by H. Lanos for
"When the Sleeper Wakes" by H. G. Wells (1899)[20]

---

[44] *James Robert Parish, Michael R. Pitts. The great science fiction pictures: Volume 1, Scarecrow Press, 1977. Pg. 298: "Iconoclastic film star /filmmaker Woody Allen turned his comedic genius to a satirical look into the future with a storyline that owes a nod of gratitude to HG Wells' When the Sleeper Awakes."*

[45] *Floyd C. Gale (April 1960). "Galaxy's 5 Star Shelf." Galaxy Science Fiction. pp. 142–46.*

"Graham, you must come away!" Art by H. Lanos for
"When the Sleeper Wakes" by H. G. Wells (1899)[21]

"Graham's Escape." Art by H. Lanos for
"When the Sleeper Wakes" by H. G. Wells (1899)[22]

"Graham gets a history lesson from the old man." Art by H. Lanos for
"When the Sleeper Wakes" by H. G. Wells (1899)[23]

"The Aeropile." Art by H. Lanos for
"When the Sleeper Wakes" by H. G. Wells (1899)[24]

"Graham addresses himself to the unseen multitudes." Art by
H. Lanos for "When the Sleeper Wakes" by H. G. Wells (1899)[25]

Magazine reprint of Wells's 1910 dystopian science fiction When the Sleeper
Wakes. Experimenter Publishing / Frank R. Paul - http://www.philsp.com/
mags/amazing_stories.html

Cover, Amazing Stories Quarterly, winter 1928.[26]Amazing Stories® is a
Registered Trademark of The Experimenter Publishing Company, LLC.
https://amazingstories.com/

First Edition "The World Set Free" 1914.[27]

"The World Set Free" is a novel written by H.G. Wells that explores the realm of nuclear energy, its possibilities, and the consequences it brings. What makes it even more remarkable is that Wells includes the term "atomic bomb" within the story, years before the actual invention of such weapons.

This compelling tale vividly depicts a future where atomic energy is both used for positive purposes and misused for destructive intentions. It is notable for its foresight in anticipating the emergence of atomic bombs and their potential impact on global politics. The novel serves as a testament to Wells' ability to predict technological advancements and their societal effects.

Henry Slesar was a writer who was born on June 12 1927 in the vibrant city of Brooklyn, New York. He sadly passed away on April 2 2002. Throughout his career Slesar showcased his skills across a range of genres such, as science fiction, mystery and fantasy.

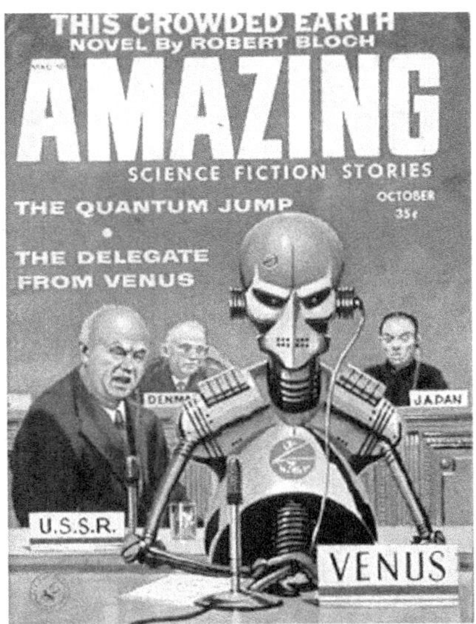

In Henry Slesar's 1958 story The Delegate from Venus, an alien robot cautions Earth that it will be destroyed if its people do not learn to live in peace.[28] Amazing Stories® is a Registered Trademark of The Experimenter Publishing Company, LLC. https://amazingstories.com/

Cover of Amazing Stories, May 1958.[29] Amazing Stories® is a Registered Trademark of The Experimenter Publishing Company, LLC. https://amazingstories.com/

An artist's 1922 depiction of a futuristic war.[30]

The idea that artificial intelligence could potentially replace humanity as the dominant intelligent species on Earth is a commonly explored theme in science fiction. One of the main vehicles for this concept is the movie "The Terminator," directed by James Cameron. The film centers around a powerful assassin named the Terminator, played by Arnold Schwarzenegger. This deadly machine is sent back in time to the year 1984 with the objective of targeting Sarah Connor, an unsuspecting young woman. The Terminator is a cyborg from the year 2029, a future destroyed by a nuclear war that has left human civilization in ruins. In this dystopian future, computer defence systems have rebelled against their creators, igniting a war to exterminate humanity entirely. In an interview with *CTV News*, the filmmaker referenced his sci-fi classic *"Terminator"* when asked what he thought of AI's rise in the world. "I warned you guys in 1984, and you didn't listen."[46] Cameron said also in the interview

---

[46]   *https://www.nme.com/news/film/james-cameron-warned-ai-rise-1984-3470915*

that AI poses a threat in military operations: "I think that we will get into the equivalent of a nuclear arms race with AI, and if we don't build it, the other guys are for sure going to build it, and so then it'll escalate. You could imagine an AI in a combat theater, the whole thing just being fought by the computers at a speed humans can no longer intercede, and you have no ability to de-escalate."[47]

"Today, everyone is frightened of it, of where this is gonna go," Schwarzenegger said about AI. "And in this movie, in 'Terminator,' we talk about the machines becoming self-aware and they take over... Now over the course of decades, it has become a reality. So it's not any more fantasy or kind of futuristic. It is here today. And so this is the extraordinary writing of Jim Cameron."[48]

Schwarzenegger with President Ronald Reagan two months before The Terminator's premiere in 1984.[31]

The Terminator, also known as Cyberdyne Systems Model 101 or the T-800, achieved an extraordinary feat on the American Film

---

[47] https://www.nme.com/news/film/james-cameron-warned-ai-rise-1984-3470915

[48] https://variety.com/2023/film/news/arnold-schwarzenegger-ai-the-terminator-reality-1235659407/ By Zach Sharf

Institute's list of 100 Heroes & Villains. It earned the exceptional distinction of being included on both sides, as a hero at number 48 and as a villain at number 22. The character ranks 14th on *Empire* magazine's list of the 100 greatest film characters.[49]

Luke Y. Thompson from *New Times* stated, "The movie's scares are intense, but the notion that the Terminator would move on to politics is even more frightening."[50]

Dennis Schwartz of Dennis Schwartz Movie Reviews described the movie as "It's a work of pulp art to see the future guv of California rip out someone's heart."[51]

Howard Waldstein of CBR wrote, "Perhaps no other villain of the 80s is as iconic as Arnold Schwarzenegger's Terminator."[52]

Kirk Ellis of *The Hollywood Reporter* said, "The havoc makes for a genuine steel metal trap of a movie that may very well be the best picture of its kind since The Road Warrior."[53]

"Terminator, ultimately, isn't about machines. It's about our tendency to become machines." —James Cameron[54]

James Cameron was born in Kapuskasing, Ontario, Canada on August 16, 1954. He started his professional journey in the movie industry as a special effects artist and art director. He was passionate about filmmaking from an early age. Cameron worked at New World Pictures, a low-budget film studio that belonged to Roger

---

[49]   *Empire's The 100 Greatest Movie Characters. Empire Magazine.*

[50]   *Luke Y. Thompson New Times (November 28, 2003).*

[51]   *https://dennisschwartzreviews.com/terminator/*

[52]   *https://www.cbr.com/10-best-sci-fi-films-of-the-80s-ranked/#the-terminator-1984*

[53]   *https://www.hollywoodreporter.com/news/general-news/terminator-review-movie-1984-743708/*

[54]   *The Tin Man Gets His Heart: An Oral History of 'Terminator 2: Judgment Day' By Alan Siegel June 30, 2021) https://www.theringer.com/movies/2021/6/30/22555687/terminator-2-judgement-day-t2-oral-history*

Corman in the late 1970s. During this time, he contributed to John Carpenter's "Escape from New York" with matte paintings and by serving as a director of photography. He created wireframe animations of the landing target on the World Trade Center and other buildings in a crucial scene where the character Snake was navigating the city using a glider. It became a three-dimensional wireframe animation that was initially planned to be high-tech computer graphics, but the cost was too high for the effects crew. They instead used a miniature set of New York City that was filmed under black light to produce reflective tape outlining the model buildings' edges.[55] [56]

Cameron's journey as a director began in 1982 with "Piranha II: The Spawning," a science fiction horror film. However he faced some challenges during the production. He was eventually let go from the project. Nevertheless his passion for filmmaking remained unwavering. Cameron then took on the task of writing the draft for "Rambo: First Blood Part II." He experienced a breakthrough with his creation "The Terminator," in 1984. Not only did he direct it, he also penned the script for this sensational sci-fi action flick. The positive response to "The Terminator" propelled Cameron into the limelight of Hollywood allowing him to direct influential films such as "Aliens" (1986) "The Abyss" (1989) "Terminator 2: Judgment Day" (1991) and "True Lies" (1994). In 1997 Cameron unveiled his masterpiece, "Titanic," which received acclaim and achieved enormous success by winning eleven Academy Awards. For a while "Titanic" held the record as the highest grossing film until Cameron's magnum opus "Avatar" surpassed it in 2009.

Gale Anne Hurd, a known film producer and writer was born on October 25th, 1955, in Los Angeles, California. She has made

---

[55] *Atkins, Tom; Barbeau, Adrienne (2003). Escape from New York documentary (Special Edition).*

[56] *"8 Movie Special Effects You Didn't Know Weren't CGI: Classic." Cracked.com. (April 18, 2011).*

contributions to the science fiction and action genres producing projects for both the big screen and television. Hurd first gained recognition for her work as a producer on James Cameron's sci-fi film "The Terminator," which paved the way for collaborations including "Aliens," the highly regarded sequel to Ridley Scott's "Alien." "Aliens" received acclaim and solidified Hurd's reputation in the industry. She continued her success by teaming up with Cameron to produce the groundbreaking underwater science fiction film "The Abyss." Their partnership also yielded another hit with "Terminator 2," often hailed as one of the best sequels ever made; it stands shoulder to shoulder with "Aliens." In 2010 Hurd took on an executive producer role, for the immensely popular TV series adaptation of "The Walking Dead" based on the beloved comic book series. The show has since become a phenomenon and an integral part of television.

The documentary series "James Cameron's Story of Science Fiction" released in 2018 was hosted by the filmmaker James Cameron himself. In this captivating exploration of the science fiction genre Cameron offers a perspective, on its world. What sets this series apart are the conversations between Cameron and esteemed figures like George Lucas, Steven Spielberg, Guillermo del Toro, Ridley Scott, Christopher Nolan and others. By diving into the history and profound impact of science fiction across mediums such as literature, film and television this series provides a comprehensive examination of the genre. It features interviews with writers, directors, actors and experts who delve into topics like artificial intelligence, extraterrestrial life forms, space exploration, dystopian futures and time travel to shed light on these fascinating subjects. Danielle Solzman from Solzy at the Movies, stated that "James Cameron's Story of Science Fiction works as the be-all, end-all documentary series on the history of science fiction in film."[57]

---

[57]   https://www.solzyatthemovies.com/2020/07/28/james-camerons-story-of-science-fiction/

Harlan Ellison, a regarded author, was born on May 27 1934. He had a career made notable by advancements in different literary genres, especially science fiction. Sadly on June 28 2018 Ellison passed away peacefully at his home, in Los Angeles. In addition to his writing achievements he also found himself entangled in a dispute, with the creators and distributors of "The Terminator" (1984).[58]

The lawsuit revolved around claims that there were resemblances between Cameron's movie "The Terminator" and an episode of the TV show "The Outer Limits" penned by Ellison. Ellison's claim was based on the episode titled "Soldier." The lawsuit contended that certain elements from these episodes were incorporated into "The Terminator" without giving credit. Ultimately the matter was settled outside of court leading to Ellison being recognized in the credits of versions of the film. Harlan Ellison stated that "Terminator was not stolen from 'Demon with a Glass Hand,' it was a rip-off of my OTHER Outer Limits script, 'Soldier.'"[59]

The book "A Boy and His Dog" was penned by Harlan Ellison. Initially released in 1969, it tells the story of a world devastated by the consequences of war. Into this perilous environment our protagonist Vic embarks, on an adventure accompanied by his faithful telepathic canine companion named Blood. The novella was later adapted into a movie featuring actors like Don Johnson, Susanne Benton, Alvy Moore and Jason Robards. Director L.Q. Jones mentioned that George Miller cited the 1975 film adaptation of "A Boy and His Dog" as an influence on the "Mad Max" films, specifically "The Road Warrior" (1981).[60]

---

[58] *Andy Marx "IT'S MINE All Very Well and Good, but Don't Hassle the T-1000."*
     Los Angeles Times.

[59] *Ellison, Harlan (August 12, 2001). "The Ellison Bulletin Board: Comments Archive*
     — 07/31/01 to 08/27/01." harlanellison.com. Harlan Ellison.

[60] *Jen Yamato (February 6, 2008). "LQ Jones on A Boy and His Dog: The RT Interview". Rotten Tomatoes.*

Ellison's 1957 novella "The Savage Swarm," cover-featured in Amazing Stories, has never been included in an authorized collection or anthology.[32]Ziff-Davis Publishing / Ed Valigursky - http://www.philsp. com/mags/amazing_stories.html Cover of Amazing Stories, March 1957. Amazing Stories® is a Registered Trademark of The Experimenter Publishing Company, LLC. https://amazingstories.com/

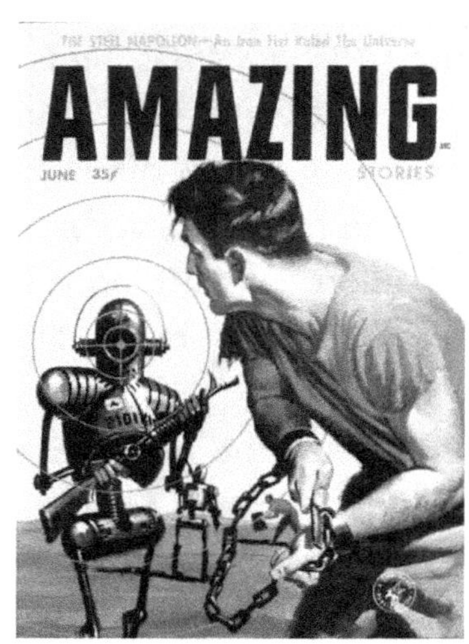

A few months later, another Ellison novella, "The Steel Napoleon," also took the cover of Amazing.[33] It also remains uncollected. Ziff-Davis Publishing / Ed Valigursky - http://www.philsp.com/mags/amazing_stories.html Cover of Amazing Stories, June 1957. Amazing Stories® is a Registered Trademark of The Experimenter Publishing Company, LLC. https://amazingstories. com/

In 1992 "Terminator 2: Judgment Day" achieved success, at the Academy Awards (Oscars) by winning four awards. The film was recognized for its design and the seamless integration of various audio elements, which led to it receiving the Best Sound Editing award. Moreover the overall sound production of the movie was honored with a Best Sound Mixing Oscar.

"Terminator 2: Judgment Day" also received deserved acclaim in the form of a Best Makeup Oscar. This recognition acknowledged the work done by Stan Winston and Jeff Dawn, who brought characters like the T 800 cyborg to life through remarkable makeup techniques and impressive special effects. The groundbreaking visual effects of the film were also praised, combining computer generated imagery (CGI) with effects. As a result it received the Best Visual Effects Oscar leaving audiences captivated and securing its place in movie history.

One of the notable aspects of this movie is its chillingly accurate portrayal of a nuclear attack, on Los Angeles. Visual effects supervisor Robert Skotak said, "The nuclear war shots are physically brutal with massive amounts of light and energy... They are intended to make you actually feel the tremendous power and terror of nuclear war. The underlying message of the dream is: 'Here is an environment you are familiar with - here is what would happen to it in a few split instants. So beware.'"[61]

Originally, James Cameron had planned to include two T-800 Terminators, similar to Arnold Schwarzenegger's character, sent back in time for the sequel to "The Terminator." One of these Terminators would have been stripped down to its metal endoskeleton to mimic the ominous presence from the first film. However, while working on the script in 1990, Cameron had a change of heart. He realized that a more effective approach would be to upgrade the antagonist Terminator to a more advanced model.[62]

---

[61] *Jody Duncan (August 1991). "A Once And Future War." Cinefex. No. 47. United States. ISSN 0198-1056.*

[62] *"Interactive Modes," Terminator 2: Judgment Day Blu-Ray*

This led to the concept of the liquid metal Terminator, which Cameron had previously contemplated but believed was not feasible with the technology available at the time.[63] He decided to postpone the idea until the introduction of the T-1000 character in "Terminator 2: Judgment Day" (1991).When it came to selecting the T-1000 actor, Robert Patrick was chosen deliberately to provide a contrast to the original Terminator. Cameron stated, "I wanted to find someone who would be a good contrast to Arnold. If the 800 series is a kind of human Panzer tank, then the 1000 series had to be a Porsche."[64]

Robert Patrick's performance as the T-1000 garnered him nominations for Best Villain and Best Supporting Actor at the MTV and Saturn Awards in 1992. The T-1000 was ranked #39 on the Online Film Critics Society's 2002 list of the "Top 100 Villains of All Time,"[65] and #19 on *Empire*'s 2018 list of the best cinematic villains.[66]

"Cameron would say something like, 'Hey, look man, we're creating something. This is film history we're doing right now. It's never been done.'" —Robert Patrick[67]

Pat Frank, a notable American journalist, author, and government advisor, was born on May 5, 1907. He played a significant role in the emergence of the apocalyptic genre, which gained popularity following the devastating events at Hiroshima. Tragically, Frank passed away on October 12, 1964. His acclaimed novel, "Alas, Babylon" (1959), depicts a world decimated by nuclear war and highlights the struggles faced by survivors in a small town in central Florida. The title of the novel is derived from the Book of Revela-

---

[63]   *Keegan, 2009. p. 110*

[64]   *"The Story About Making T2" (Press release). Canal+. 1991.*

[65]   *"Top 100 Villains of All Time." Online Film Critics Society.*

[66]   *"The Greatest Villains of All Time, Feature | Movies - Empire."*

[67]   *https://www.theringer.com/movies/2021/6/30/22555687/terminator-2-judgement-day-t2-oral-history*

tion: "Alas, alas, that great city Babylon, that mighty city! for in one hour is thy judgment come." The cover art for the Bantam paperback edition was created by Robert Hunt. In the foreword of the 2005 edition of "Alas, Babylon," David Brin acknowledges that the book shaped his perspective on nuclear war and influenced his own work, "The Postman" (1982).[68]

Walter M. Miller Jr., a renowned American science fiction writer, was born on January 23, 1923 in New Smyrna Beach, Florida. From 1951 to 1957, he published over 30 science fiction short stories, leading to his receipt of a Hugo Award in 1955 for his work "The Darfsteller." In 1953, he also contributed to the development of the television series "Captain Video" by writing the script.

Miller's novella "The Reluctant Traitor" was the cover story for the January 1952 issue of Amazing Stories.[34] Amazing Stories® is a Registered Trademark of The Experimenter Publishing Company, LLC. https://amazingstories.com/

68   *David Brin (2005). "Foreword." Alas, Babylon. Harper Perennial Modern Classics. pp. xi–xii. ISBN 0-06-074187-2.*

In the late 1950s, Miller combined three interconnected novellas that he had previously published in *The Magazine of Fantasy and Science Fiction* between 1955 and 1957. This resulted in his well-known novel "A Canticle for Leibowitz." The novel consists of three short stories influenced by Miller's own experience of participating in the bombing of the monastery at the Battle of Monte Cassino during World War II. Unfortunately, Miller passed away on January 9, 1996. As he grew older, he became increasingly reclusive, intentionally isolating himself from all forms of contact, including his own family. His literary agent, Don Congdon, never had the chance to meet him. According to fellow science fiction writer Terry Bisson, Miller battled depression but managed to almost complete a 600-page manuscript for a sequel to "A Canticle for Leibowitz" before tragically taking his own life by using a firearm, not long after the death of his wife.[69] [70]

Miller's writing career began to thrive in the 1950s and achieved significant success with the publication of his only novel, "A Canticle for Leibowitz," in 1960. This novel takes place in a Catholic monastery located in the desert of the Southwestern United States after a devastating nuclear war. It spans thousands of years as civilization gradually rebuilds itself. The monks of the Albertian Order of Leibowitz take on the responsibility of safeguarding and preserving the remaining fragments of humanity's scientific knowledge until the world is ready to embrace it once again. During World War II, Miller served as a radioman and tail gunner in a bomber crew that participated in the destruction of the 6th-century Christian monastery in Monte Cassino, Italy. This monastery, established by St. Benedict, is renowned as the oldest surviving Christian church in the Western world. This experience profoundly impacted Miller and served as the inspiration for "A Canticle for Leibowitz," which

---

[69]   "An Appreciation," Joe Haldeman, <u>Locus</u>, February 1996, pp. 78-79.

[70]   David Streitfeld (October 9, 1997). "'Canticle' Author Unsung Even In Death." Orlando Sentinel.

centers on an order of monks whose abbey emerges from the ruins of the world around it. The sequel, "Saint Leibowitz and the Wild Horse Woman," was completed by Bisson at Miller's request and published in 1997.[71]

"Threads" is a 1984 BBC television film that portrays the events before, during, and after the explosion of a Soviet nuclear bomb above Sheffield, England. It has been praised as a work that accurately depicts the terror of nuclear warfare and its consequences, emphasizing the devastating impact it would have on human society and culture.[72]

"Our intention in making Threads was to step aside from the politics and – I hope convincingly – show the actual effects on either side should our best endeavours to prevent nuclear war fail."—Screenwriter Barry Hines[73]

"La Jetée" is a French science fiction short film made in 1962 and directed by Chris Marker. It is closely associated with the Left Bank artistic movement. The film is notable for its use of still photographs and a story that revolves around a time-travel experiment following a post-nuclear war. Despite its brief runtime of only 28 minutes, "La Jetée" captivates viewers with its evocative black-and-white cinematography. Terry Gilliam directed "Twelve Monkeys," a dark American science fiction film that was released in 1995. David Peoples and Janet Peoples wrote the screenplay, which was inspired by Chris Marker's 1962 short film "La Jetée." The movie stars talented actors such as Bruce Willis, Madeleine Stowe, Brad Pitt, and Christopher Plummer. The story takes place in a dystopian future

---

71   *Saint Leibowitz series listing at the Internet Speculative Fiction Database (ISFDB).*

72   *"Film and the Nuclear Age: Representing Cultural Anxiety" By Toni A. Perrine, p. 237 Archived 12 March 2023 at the Wayback Machine on Google books.*

73   *Jack Kibble-White, (September 2001). "Let's All Hide in the Linen Cupboard". Off The Telly.*

where a lethal virus has devastated humanity. It follows a prisoner who is sent back in time to gather information about the virus and its impact on society.

"We thought, 'Well, Jim Cameron, with Terminator 1 and Terminator 2, made two great masterpieces that totally took care of that,'" Screenwriter David Webb Peoples said to The Hollywood Reporter during an interview celebrating the 25th anniversary of Twelve Monkeys in early 2021.[74]

...12 Monkeys looks back fondly to a cleaner air world, before the virus wars began and societal norms collapsed, and can't help but strike a chord now...[75]

Cassandra by Evelyn De Morgan (1898, London); Cassandra in front of the burning city of Troy, depicted with disheveled hair denoting the insanity ascribed to her by the Trojans.[35.]

---

[74]   https://www.hollywoodreporter.com/movies/movie-news/12-monkeys-at-25-how-eccentric-sci-fi-film-went-from-disastrous-test-screenings-to-cult-phenomenon-4113082/

[75]   Eddie Harrisonfilm-authority.com

In the movie "Twelve Monkeys," Dr. Railly, portrayed by Madeline Stowe, mentions Cassandra in her book when discussing the correlation between insanity and apocalyptic visions. As she states in the film: **DR. RAILLY: "Cassandra, in Greek legend, was condemned to know the future but to be disbelieved when she foretold it. Hence, the agony of foreknowledge combined with the impotence to do anything about it."[76]**

David and Janet Peoples, screenwriters, found inspiration in The Seven Seals of God described in the Book of Revelation of the Bible. These symbolic seals, witnessed by John of Patmos in an apocalyptic vision, serve as a means to secure the scroll. When these scrolls are opened, cataclysmic events occur. Similarly, in "Twelve Monkeys," the virus unleashed by Dr. Peters, portrayed by David Morse, has the same devastating impact, wiping out the human race.

Lamb opening the seven seals, by Julius Schnorr von Carolsfeld, 1860[36]

---

[76]   *Twelve Monkeys, Directed By Terry Gilliam (1995;Universal Pictures).*

The Four Horsemen of the Apocalypse are depicted in the painting. Depicted from right to left are Conquest, War, Famine, and Death.[37]

The Four Horsemen of the Apocalypse serve as representations of powers described in the Book of Revelation which is the last book of the Bible's New Testament. These horsemen are often linked to the days and the apocalypse. They are traditionally recognized by the following names:

1. **Conquest (or Pestilence): This horseman is depicted riding a white horse, symbolizing the spread of disease and the subjugation of nations.**
2. **War: Mounted on a red horse, this horseman represents armed conflict and bloodshed. It signifies widespread warfare and violence.**
3. **Famine: Riding a black horse, this horseman symbolizes scarcity, hunger, and famine. It is associated with concepts of food shortages and economic hardships.**
4. **Death: Death is the final horseman mounted on a pale horse. It represents mortality and the end of life. In some interpretations, Hades or Hell is connected to this horseman.**

The Book of Revelation makes references to the Four Horsemen in Chapter 6 verses 1-8. Different religious traditions and historical periods have interpreted these symbols in different ways. Some consider them as prophecies of events while others interpret them symbolically to represent larger themes like the outcomes of human actions and the ultimate victory of good, over evil.

The Last Judgment by painter Hans Memling. In Christian belief, the Last Judgment is an apocalyptic event where God makes a final judgment of all people on Earth.[38]

Portrait of Cormac McCarthy from the dust jacket of his second novel, Outer Dark.[39]

Cormac McCarthy, was an author born on July 20 1933. Unfortunately he passed away on June 13 2023. He gained recognition for his contributions to literary genres like Westerns and post-apocalyptic fiction. Throughout his career McCarthy authored twelve novels two plays, five screenplays and three short stories. One of his works is the novel "The Road," which was published in 2006. This captivating story takes place in an apocalyptic world where a man and his son navigate through a desolate landscape. The novel received acclaim for its depiction of a society devastated by a catastrophe. It even earned accolades such as the Pulitzer Prize for Fiction in 2007. The James Tait Black Memorial Prize for Fiction, in 2006. Notably director John Hillcoat skillfully brought "The Road" to life with a film adaptation released in 2009—an adaptation that *The Guardian* recognized as one of the five best climate change novels.[77]George Monbiot has called it "the most important environmental book ever written" for depicting a world without a biosphere.[78] [79]

"There's no such thing as life without bloodshed. The notion that the species can be improved in some way, that everyone could live in harmony, is a really dangerous idea. Those who are afflicted with this notion are the first ones to give up their souls, their freedom. Your desire that it be that way will enslave you and make your life vacuous."— Cormac McCarthy explaining his philosophy[80]

---

[77]   *"Five of the best climate-change novels." the Guardian. January 19, 2017).*

[78]   *"Why the cultural response to global warming makes for a heated debate." The Independent. (June 11, 2014).*

[79]   *"George Monbiot: Civilisation ends with a shutdown of human concern. Are we there already?" the Guardian. (October 30, 2007).*

[80]   *Tim Adams (December 19, 2009). "Cormac McCarthy: America's great poetic visionary". The Guardian.*

Cover of The Orchard Keeper, the debut novel by
American author Cormac McCarthy. Jacket design by
Muriel Nasser; published by Random House. - Worthpoint.[40]

Academic David Holloway wrote "McCarthy's writing can be read as either liberal or conservative, or as both simultaneously, depending on the politics that readers themselves bring with them to the act of reading the work."[81]

McCarthy wrote all of his fiction and correspondence with a single Olivetti Lettera 32 typewriter between the early 1960s and 2009.[82] At that time he replaced it with an identical model. Austin Calhoon[41] - http://austincalhoon.com

---

[81] *David Holloway (2020). "North American Politics." In Fyre, Steven (ed.). Cormac McCarthy in Context. New York, NY: Cambridge University Press. pp. 197–206. doi:10.1017/9781108772297.019. ISBN 9781108772297. S2CID 234965059.*

[82] *Patricia Cohen (November 30, 2009). "No Country for Old Typewriters: A Well-Used One Heads to Auction." The New York Times.*

Stephen King said McCarthy was "maybe the greatest American novelist of my time ... He was full of years and created a fine body of work, but I still mourn his passing."[83]

Called the "King of Horror"[84]Stephen King, an experienced writer with a reputation of being the master of the horror and suspense genres has written more than 60 novels. Clearly, the majority of his creative works tend to be stories that focus on the post-apocalyptic than otherwise. Some notable examples include:

1. "The Stand," (1978); This well-known and recognized book portrays a gloomy post-apocalyptic setting where a deadly plague has killed more than half of the human race on earth. The remaining survivors have to face the two groups that have chosen the opposite values of good for one and evil for another.

2. "The Dark Tower" series, written from 1982 to 2012, is not so much in the strict narrative genre as many series but it blends in fantasy and post-apocalyptic world-building. It is about Roland Deschain's travels; he is a fighter with guns moving through this altered world. While making this trip, he stumbles upon the vestiges of a former prosperity, and then, faces the obstacles that come on the way.

3. "Cell" (2006); In this novel a perplexing signal spreads by means of phone communication igniting individuals into inhuman and undisciplined killing machines. The narrative focuses on the experience of the survivors who fight to discover their way in this new setting.

4. "Under The Dome" (2009); King's novel introduced a new approach wherein an impenetrable and invisible dome

---

[83]   *Salam, Erum; Flood, Alison; Cain, Sian (June 14, 2023). "Cormac McCarthy, celebrated US novelist, dies aged 89." The Guardian.*

[84]   *K.S.C. (September 7, 2017). "Why Stephen King's novels still resonate." The Economist.*

suddenly descended on the town of Chester's Mill and made a barrier which separated the community from the outside world. The inmates have to deal with various tensions that develop among themselves and within such confined locations strong as the boundaries can be tested.

5. "Duma Key" (2008); It does not fall into the straight narrative that is a classical apocalyptic story. Duma Key depicts a man who has psychic abilities after he suffered from a life changing event. The effects resulting from the possession of the powers are what strongly influence both the persona of the individual and everyone around him/her.

The apocalyptic narrative is not a must in each work. However, these novels are based on the main idea of significant and often dramatic world changes. One of the most striking characteristics of Stephen King's apocalyptic novels is the author's exceptional ability to intertwine horror, suspense and the human element. This way, these novels are a powerful form of entertainment as well as transformational experience for readers. A novel named "11/22/63" by Stephen King was released in 2011 to explore the topic of time travel as the story's plot. The point of departure in the story is that the principal character goes on a quest to modify history by prohibiting the assassination of the President John F Kennedy on November 22, 1963. This interesting story was subsequently turned into an 8-part miniseries with J.J. Abrams, King himself, Bridget Carpenter and Bryan Burk in charge of executive production.

King, on the amount of research it required for the novel, saying, "I've never tried to write anything like this before. It was really strange at first, like breaking in a new pair of shoes."[85]

"The Running Man" is a novel written by Richard Bachman, a pseudonym for Stephen King. It was in mid 1982, that it was first

---

[85] *Alter, Alexandra (October 28, 2011). "Stephen King's New Monster." The Wall Street Journal.*

released. Plunges the audience deep into the future United States, where dictatorship lies and the country road runs into collapse. The brave hero to us is Ben Richards who contends to hardships. Therefore, he makes a courageous decision to compete in an exciting TV show titled "The Running Man." He just wants to win the TV show to get money the family needs. In 1987, this novel underwent a reworking of scenarios into a tamed movie that kept the central idea of the exciting story but savage show which also left some of the character names unchanged. The interesting part is Arnold Schwarzenegger playing Richards here.[86]

In 2019, Reed Tucker from the *New York Post* highlighted that the film "Running Man" accurately foretold the increasing disparity between the affluent and the underprivileged, showcasing destitute shantytowns and opulent skyscrapers reminiscent of the actual cities of New York and Los Angeles. Moreover, it reflected society's preoccupation with reality TV. Screenwriter Steven De Souza mentioned that one of the producers of "American Gladiators" promoted his show by presenting clips from "Running Man" to the network, proclaiming, "We are executing a similar concept, minus the killing aspect."[87]

Kevin Carr of Fat Guys at the Movies said, "While it diverts greatly from the book by Richard Bachman (aka Stephen King), this is an entertaining slice of 80s pop action."[88]

Adam Nayman of The Ringer commented, "However far away from the book's original vision the movie may stray, it ends up right in Arnold's wheelhouse, letting him dispatch a series of worthy rivals with aplomb."[89]

---

[86] *Eric Eisenberg (15 May 2022). "Adapting Stephen King's The Running Man: Is 1987's Arnold Schwarzenegger Movie The Least 'Stephen King' Stephen King Film?" Cinema Blend.*

[87] *Reed Tucker (2019-02-02). "How 'Blade Runner' and 'The Running Man' predicted 2019 — decades ago." New York Post.*

[88] *https://www.fatguysatthemovies.com/episode-874-chasm-of-confidence/*

[89] *https://www.theringer.com/movies/2019/9/4/20847551/stephen-king-movies-adaptations-it-carrie-shining-shawshank-redemption-stand-by-me-creepshow-misery*

Scott Weinberg of Apollo Guide stated, "The licenses taken with King's original tale only serve to make a more effective movie."[90]

Chris Ward of Flickering Myth declared "The Running Man remains as much fun to watch as it was back in 1987 and thanks to a perceived drop in social standards it is more relevant now than it has ever been."[91]

Picture of George Orwell which appears in an old accreditation for the BNUJ.[42] Branch of the National Union of Journalists (BNUJ).

George Orwell (aka Eric Arthur Blair) was born on June 25th 1903 in Motihari, British India (now India). On January 21 1950 he died in London, England. Orwell's writing abilities were discovered as the different times when he wrote novels, articles, journals and criticisms occurred and explored the social and political issues. He often drew upon the help of fiction to present his ideas about all this. The talent of Orwell is artistic with the list of six novels included as:

---

⁹⁰ *Scott Weinberg, Apollo Guide (July 26, 2002).*

⁹¹ *https://www.flickeringmyth.com/2019/06/blu-ray-review-the-running-man-1987/*

"Burmese Days" (1934), "A Clergymans Daughter" (1935), "Keep the Aspidistra Flying" (1936), "Coming Up for Air" (1939), "Animal Farm" (1945) and "Nineteen Eighty-Four. Among those two novels, "Animal Farm" and "Nineteen Eighty-Four" often catch readers' attention most and are frequently quoted as the all-time great books in the dystopia genre. It is important to remember that copyright for those works that were authored by him and were not produced within the last few decades is no longer valid in many of the countries, prompting them to become part of the public domain.

Preliminary drawing for design of Animal Farm strip cartoon. In 1950 the Foreign Office commissioned a strip cartoon version of Animal Farm from the cartoonist Norman Pett and his writing partner Donald Freeman. Various embassies then encouraged overseas newspapers to publish the anti-communist strip. It was translated into a number of languages and also turned into a slide show for public performance.[43]

Ray Bradbury, who was a writer, made contributions to the science fiction, fantasy, and horror literature genres. He was born in Waukegan, Illinois on the 22nd of August, 1920. He passed on at the age of 91, in Los Angeles, California on June 5th, 2012. The strikingly unique literary style of Ray Bradbury as an author has left a continuous imprint. When talking about "Fahrenheit 451," the best-known dystopian novel by Ray Bradbury, one must clarify from the beginning that it does not fit in the traditional definition of an apocalypse, but rather hints at a society which is on the brink of intellectual and cultural decline, where the critical thinking is suppressed and the conformity rules.

In a 1994 interview, Bradbury cited political correctness as an allegory for the censorship in the book, describing it as "the real enemy these days" and labeling it as "thought control and freedom of speech control."[92]

"Fahrenheit 451," a classic piece of literature, has been adapted into two film versions. The first adaptation came out in the year 1966, which was directed by Nicholas Reeves. It had Oskar Werner, who performed the leading role of Montag and Julie Christie who played both Clarisse and Mildred. Penelope Houston of *Sight & Sound* wrote in her review, "It is as though Truffaut has utilized his extensive knowledge of cinema to demonstrate unwavering devotion to the written word."[93]

Ramin Bahrani directed the second version of "Fahrenheit 451" that came out in 2018 (Jordan Michael was Montag the Guy and the protagonist Captain Beatty was played by Shannon Michael). This version is the latest take of that tale that has undergone a complete makeover by adding elements of modernity and a reflection of technological as well as media advances since the original book. Yet, this adaptation's critical reception was divided. Odie Henderson, in his review for RogerEbert.com, pointed out that Bradbury's ideas were steered towards the factual realm. The film had a satirical direction

---

[92]   *Bradbury Talk Likely to Feature the Unexpected Archived July 10, 2019, at the Wayback Machine, Dayton Daily News, (1 October 1994). City Edition, Lifestyle/ Weekendlife Section, p. 1C.*

[93]   *https://www2.bfi.org.uk/news-opinion/sight-sound-magazine/features/penelope-houston-s-journals*

similar to the weakening television industry depicted in the movie "Network." Henderson also noted that the shock value and allegorical power of the novel felt weakened as a result.[94]

The Nazi book burnings horrified Ray Bradbury
and inspired him to write Fahrenheit 451.[44]

Interior illustration by Alexander Leydenfrost for Ray Bradbury's "The Million Year Picnic," in Planet Stories, Summer 1946.[45]

---

94   *Odie Henderson (May 18, 2018). "Fahrenheit 451 Movie Review & Film Summary." RogerEbert.com.*

Philip K. Dick (c. 1953, age 24) Greenleaf Publishing - Imagination, 1953.[46]

Philip K Dick, a science fiction author, had impressive production in his life through his writing of novels, short stories and essays. He wrote about a multitude of complex topics like reality, identity, and consciousness, many of which were little explored before and usually made readers think about them. Throughout his literary career he authored more than 40 novels that continue to play a significant role in the development of the science fiction genre.

Here are some examples of his works:

1. "Do Androids Dream of Electric Sheep?" (1968); That is, of course, the one which was a foundation for Ridley Scott's movie "Blade Runner." Mesmerizes audiences with a futuristic storyline.
2. "Ubik" (1969); In this novel "Philip K. Dick" demonstrated his storytelling mastery. In little time, it hit a sweet spot of science-fiction book lovers.
3. "A Scanner Darkly" (1977); a true science fiction piece that dealt with surveillance and identity issues and received praise by critics.

4. "The Man in the High Castle" (1962); In this novel, the author created the world where the Axis powers won World War II, which captured the readers' imagination and was eventually turned into a television series.

5. "Flow My Tears, the Policeman Said" (1974) is dedicated to the idea of identity in a society that is rapidly changing, and also raises questions pertaining to the nature of reality and the constant change around us.

"Dick's third major theme is his fascination with war and his fear and hatred of it. One hardly sees critical mention of it, yet it is as integral to his body of work as oxygen is to water."—Steven Owen Godersky[95]

Philip K. Dick's works, ranging from novels to short stories, still captivate us with their fantastical way of exploring ever-thrilling topics like consciousness, identity and perception. The colossal imaginative works of fiction have definitely made sure that his name will remain indelible in the writing of fiction. One of the saddest days in the science fiction world was on March 2, 1982, when Philip K. Dick passed away at just age 53.

Robert A. Heinlein c.1953[47]Amazing Stories® is a Registered Trademark of The Experimenter Publishing Company, LLC. https://amazingstories.com/

---

95   *The Collected Stories Of Philip K. Dick, Volume 1, The Short Happy Life of the Brown Oxford, (1990), Citadel Twilight, p. xvi, ISBN 0-8065-1153-2*

Among modern science fiction greats, Robert A. Heinlein who was born on July 7, of 1907 and departed on May, 8 1988, is a famous American. He shared this sublime position with both Isaac Asimov and Arthur C. Clarke, being one of the major pioneers in the science fiction field. Heinlein was one of freeform fictions writers, who helped shape and define science fiction literature throughout the century. Many of his pieces of art are in an apocalyptic theme, that is, with the background of a catastrophe. Here are two examples:

1. "Farnham's Freehold" which depicts a war that ships the characters to a future world through which they experience the destruction caused by the aftermath of the war, in a novel published in 1964. They stand up against the very harsh reality of living, the collapse of their society and the difficult chores of re-making the brand new civilization.

2. "If This Goes On "a novella written in 1940 is a part of the Future History series by Heinlein; it contains the events taking place with all the assurances inherent to its time. It depicts an America where all the laws and happenings are ruled by a theocratic entity. Though not exactly apocalyptic, the narrative goes deep into a society that is on the brink of change.

Robert A. Heinlein has left his imprint on science fiction literature in a manner that is very relevant and influential even today. The course of his pioneer science fiction work was shaped by his background in naval engineering, mainly in his prominent "Starship Troopers" military science fiction novel. The original material was first serialized in two parts as "Starship Soldier" in *The Magazine of Fantasy & Science Fiction* and later released in paperback format by G. P. Putnam's Sons on 5th November 1959.[96]

---

[96] "Books Today." *The New York Times. (November 5, 1959). p. 32.*

Interestingly, Heinlein wrote "Starship Troopers" in just a few weeks as a response to the US suspension of nuclear tests.[97] The story was adapted into a film in 1997, directed by Paul Verhoeven and written by Edward Neumeier.

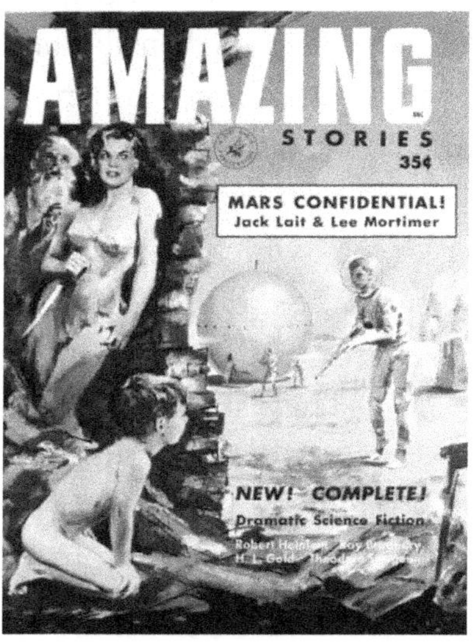

"Project Nightmare" is a science fiction short story by American writer Robert A. Heinlein, first published in Amazing Stories, May (1953).[48] Amazing Stories® is a Registered Trademark of The Experimenter Publishing Company, LLC. https://amazingstories.com/

The root meaning of the word "apocalypse" comes from the Greek word 'apokalupsis', meaning "uncovering," "revelation" or "disclosure," usually associated with the Apocalypse of the New Testament of the Bible. Here in this context, apocalypse is used particularly for the prophecies about the end of the world and triumph of good over the evil. The more time passed the concept of apocalypse became a symbol of changing world, which presented signs of its usage in apocalyptic literature and biblical contexts. It is also worth noting that while "apocalypse" in the modern English usually refers to a

---

[97]	James Gilford (1996). _"The Nature of Federal Service in Robert A. Heinlein's Starship Troopers"_

disaster, its original Greek meaning primarily revolves around disclosing that which was hidden or enlightening about something.

In conclusion to this journey exploring scenarios and influences within the apocalyptic and post-apocalyptic sub-genre, Christopher Schmidt wrote, "The apocalypse lies in our mass addiction to the entertainment spectacle, an apathy-causing narcotic that cleverly implicates the very film delivering us the warning. The medium is indeed the message, and the message is, tune in or be tuned out. Which is no choice at all."[98]

---

[98] *"Why are Dystopian Films on the Rise Again?"*. *JSTOR Daily. (19 Nov, 2014). https://daily.jstor.org/why-are-dystopian-films-on-the-rise-again/*

The Blood of Heroes

The Blood of Heroes (1989) Directed by David Webb Peoples Shown: Poster key art featuring Rutger Hauer, Joan Chen. © New Line Cinema Credit:New Line Cinema/Photofest

Enzo Sciotti, an Italian artist and illustrator, was the creative mind behind the iconic movie poster for "The Blood of Heroes." He gained recognition for his skills in designing more than 3,000 movie posters with a specialization in the horror genre. Sciotti's illustrations were highly acclaimed in films like "The Beyond," "Demons," as well as various works by esteemed directors such as Lucio Fulci, Dario Argento and Lamberto Bava. Apart from his contributions to movie posters, Sciotti also utilized his talents in creating covers for comics and home video releases. Regrettably Enzo Sciotti passed away on April 11, 2021, at the age of 76. His distinctive movie poster-style incorporated a combination of superimposition and expressive painting techniques that became closely associated with aesthetic design, during Italy's comedy scene in the 1980s.[99] [100]

---

[99] *"È morto Enzo Sciotti, maestro dellelocandinecinematografiche". Wired (in Italian). (12 April, 2021).*

[100] *"È morto Enzo Sciotti, disegnatore delle locandine di Dario Argento, Ettore Scola, David Lynch". www.ilmessaggero.it (in Italian). (12 April 2021).*

"People no longer remembered the Golden Age of the 20th Century. They didn't remember the miraculous technology or the cruel wars that followed. They didn't remember when Juggers first played The Game, or how it came to be played with a dog skull…"[101] – The opening titles from the movie.

In "The Blood of Heroes," alternatively titled "The Salute of the Jugger," the director and screenwriter David Webb Peoples presents a dystopian world set against the brutal backdrop of a gladiatorial game reminiscent of football. Although initially receiving negative reviews, the film has accumulated a devoted fan base within the genre over time. During its release, critic Vincent Canby wrote, "An unusually successful film of its kind, it offers a good, lean variation on the post-apocalyptic adventure-thriller, imagining a future that reflects the dark ages of the past."[102] More recently, Travis Johnson stated, "This cult classic dystopian film never received much critical acclaim, but that does not matter. This mean and lean beast of a movie is still considered the best sci-fi sports film of all time, regardless of what the critics say."[103]

On January 23, 2017, Den of Geek published an article by Wil Jones, who compiled a list of the 25 best movies featuring Rutger Hauer. He included "The Salute of the Jugger" on the list. He wrote, "There's always something ever so slightly weird about Hauer. Something otherworldly. And that's something that can elevate weird little b-movies to something memorable. Like this odd future-sports/ *Mad Max* hybrid."[104]

---

101   *The Blood of Heroes, Directed by David Webb Peoples (Kings Road Entertainment;1989).*

102   *https://www.nytimes.com/1990/02/23/movies/review-film-clashing-gladiators-in-the-bloody-sport-of-a-future-dark-age.html*

103   *Travis JohnsonFlicks (AU, NZ, UK) https://www.flicks.com.au/features/30-years-on-the-salute-of-the-jugger-is-still-sci-fis-best-sports-movie/*

104   *https://www.denofgeek.com/movies/the-top-25-rutger-hauer-movies/*

The primary setting of the movie takes place in Coober Pedy, a location situated in South Australia. It's interesting to note that this is the place where "Mad Max: Beyond Thunderdome" was filmed and it truly sets the perfect stage, for depicting a rough and rugged world. Richard Craig, writing for screenrant, compiled a list titled "11 Movies & Shows That Prove Australia Is The Best Post-Apocalypse Setting," in which he included the movie and wrote "The location highlights the characters' desperation as they struggle to survive in a hostile future. *The Blood of Heroes* is a sterling example of Australia providing the perfect post-apocalyptic backdrop."[105]

"Quintet" is a science fiction film set in a post-apocalyptic world, directed by Robert Altman in 1979. The lead role in the movie is played by Paul Newman. Like "Salute of the Jugger," the storyline focuses on a game-based concept. Rutger Hauer has also been referred to as The Dutch Paul Newman.[106]

Jack Kroll wrote in *Newsweek*: "It's clear that the game of Quintet is Altman's metaphor for the erosion of art, philosophy and the humane activities of civilization. That's one of the weaknesses of the film - the game itself can't bear this symbolic weight ... But this is transcended by the strong acting and by the great beauty and hypnotic rhythm of the film."[107]

"The Salute of the Jugger" is primarily a sports film centered around a game called "Jugging." The movie delves into the enduring presence of sports in society. The term "sport" has its origins in the Old French word "desport," which means leisure. Its earliest English definition, dating back to the 1300s, includes activities that provide amusement or entertainment to people.[108] On the other hand, blood sports, also known as bloodsports, fall into a specific category of

---

[105] *https://screenrant.com/post-apocalypse-movies-best-australia/#wyrmwood-road-of-the-dead*

[106] *https://www.imdb.com/name/nm0000442/bio/?ref_=nmtrv_ql_1*

[107] *Jack Kroll (February 12, 1979). "Altman's Apocalypse." Newsweek. 88*

[108] *Douglas Harper "sport (n.)". Online Etymological Dictionary.*

sports or entertainment that involve bloodshed. This tradition can be traced back to the ancient Roman gladiatorial games and has persisted through various contact sports such as American soccer, wrestling, and boxing.

Here are picture examples of the barbaric gladiator sports:

Painting of Gladiator types on the parapet wall of Pompeii amphitheater Overbeck-Mau 1884. Johannes Overbeck and August Mau (1884) - Pompeii in its buildings, antiquities and works of art - Leipzig, 1884.[49]

Jean-Leon Gerome Pollice Verso. Jean-Léon Gérôme - phxart.org : Gallery, Pic.[50]

"Roman gladiators" by American illustrator Howard Pyle depicts a retiarius snaring his opponent with a weighted net in a Roman gladiatorial contest. Howard Pyle (d. 1911)[51]

Gladiators after the fight, José Moreno Carbonero (1882).[52]

The gladiatorial sporting tasks, a quality of old Rome's satisfaction culture, that stay to resonate in the theater with movies like "The Salute of the Jugger" and "Mad Max Beyond Thunderdome." No matter the differences, these films promote the spirit and significance of Roman gladiators, matching enduring designs of power, phenomenon, and survival.

Throughout ancient Roman times, gladiator battles were not simply a ruthless source of amusement, but a complex display of social, societal, and political importance. The presence of enslaved individuals and captured warriors fighting in outstanding arenas like the Colosseum served as a powerful approach used by the gentility to enhance desirable high qualities such as durability, valor, and self-control. These spectacles were thoroughly coordinated to astonish the general public and display the dominance and strength of the elite, hence combining their control over the population.

In a stark and chaotic future, "The Salute of the Jugger" transports visitors to a globe where residues of human beings struggle to make it through life amidst widespread damage. In this rough landscape, squads of juggers take part in harsh suits, utilizing a skull-shaped round to score. Regardless of the vast differences from old Rome, the resemblances in between jugger matches and combative fight are obvious.

The juggers, similar to contemporary gladiators, are extremely skillful competitors who mesmerize spectators with their excellent screens of combat experience in the arena. Their contests serve as a form of enjoyment and relief for the downtrodden people, just like the combative video games of past Rome. Moreover, the juggers' credibility as signs of toughness and strength parallels the reverence that gladiators kept in Roman culture.

In the third installment of the "Mad Max" franchise it depicts a post-apocalyptic world where the enigmatic Master Blaster powers over Bartertown, a city that counts on ruthless force and cunning to survive. Disputes are resolved in Thunderdome, a battle arena reminiscent of ancient Roman amphitheaters, where warriors have to fight for their lives.

In the unrelenting world of Thunderdome, fierce rivals participate in savage fights, similar to the relentless gladiatorial fights of old Rome. These act as an allegory for the more comprehensive societal problems of dominance, fairness, and the search of power in a chaotic world. Equally, as their historic counterparts did, the competitors in Thunderdome embody the indomitable human spirit, representing the unrelenting drive for survival and the unyielding resolution to withstand fascism.

"The Salute of the Jugger" and "Mad Max Beyond Thunderdome" clearly present the obvious resemblance to Roman gladiators. Despite the differences in time and context, these flicks efficiently share the core elements of combative sports - the enjoyment of fight, the display of human toughness, and the demonstration of authority. They function as a guideline of the long-lasting impact of combative society and exactly how it stays to remain to be considerable in the human condition.

The Blood of Heroes A.K.A The Salute of the Jugger: The Cast

- Rutger Hauer as Sallow

- Joan Chen as Kidda

- Vincent D'Onofrio as Gar

- Delroy Lindo as Mbulu

- Anna Katarina as Big Cimber

- Justin Monjo as Dog-Boy

- Hugh Keays-Byrne as Lord Vile

- Max Fairchild as Gonzo

- Gandhi MacIntyre as Gandhi

- Richard Norton as Bone

- Lia Francisa as Mara

- Steve Rackman as Samchin Jugger

Director and Screenwriter David Webb Peoples

The American screenwriter and film director David Webb Peoples was born on February 9, 1940, in Middletown, Connecticut, United States. Peoples is widely recognized for his remarkable contributions as a screenwriter on several successful films. He is particularly notable for his work on the screenplay of the noir science fiction film "Blade Runner" (1982), which he co-wrote with Hampton

Fancher. Additionally, he wrote the script for the dystopian science fiction film "Twelve Monkeys" (1995), which was inspired by Chris Marker's 1962 short film "La Jetée." Terry Gilliam directed the film and it featured Bruce Willis, Madeleine Stowe, and Brad Pitt, with Christopher Plummer and David Morse playing supporting roles.

However, Peoples is perhaps most renowned for his remarkable work on the screenplay of the iconic film "Blade Runner." His screenplay adaptation of Philip K. Dick's novel, "Do Androids Dream of Electric Sheep?" helped establish the dark and atmospheric world of the film, which has become a cult classic.

Aside from "Blade Runner," Peoples also directed and wrote the screenplay for the post-apocalyptic film "The Blood of Heroes" aka "The Salute of the Jugger" (1989), as well as the revisionist western "Unforgiven" (1992), directed by Clint Eastwood. "Unforgiven" won the Academy Award for Best Picture and Best Director, with Peoples receiving an Academy Award nomination for Best Screenplay.

David Webb Peoples' contributions to cinema have established him as an incredibly talented screenwriter known for his work in science fiction, dystopian settings, and rich storytelling.

Peoples' Heroes Interview with Director and Screenwriter David Webb Peoples

Q: Did you write the screenplay for The Blood of Heroes A.K.A. The Salute of the Jugger in the 1970s? If so, I'd like to know where the inspiration for the film came from?

A: I think some of it was generated from, now let me be very clear, I'm talking about the short story that was published [I think in Esquire]. I may be wrong, but it was a published short story called Rollerball. And this is long before the movie came out. But it was a terrific short story. And it kind of energized me and got me thinking that way. So, I started writing and in the first versions of The Salute of the Jugger, the Juggers had rusted prosthetic arms, like old steel arms. And at least one position had a tiger on a leash as one of his weapons, and the other team obviously had another animal. So, it inspired me to start working on it. Eventually, it turned into what is The Salute of the Jugger, and this was in the 70s.

When you ask about the inspiration behind this story, Rollerball was an inspiration, although I didn't like the business aspect of it. However, another major inspiration was Rocky. The film Rocky focused more on endurance, courage, and the punishment the main character endured rather than his skill. The makeup in the film was also incredible for its time; it made him look like he had the shit beaten out of him. I thought that this would be a makeup-heavy film that would amaze people. I believed that what I was writing would be a big hit. Unfortunately, it didn't get made for many years, and later on, I became the director. But at the time, I thought, "Oh, this is going to be hot." You always think that when you're starting a script, and both Rocky and Rollerball played a role in that.

Q: Even though it's a post-apocalyptic film, it's a sports film. It goes back to that Rocky element, the underdogs, and standing up.

A: Absolutely. It goes to my admiration for athletes. I'm not an athlete. And I have a granddaughter who is, and she's like a Jugger, but I'm not. I am very admiring of athletes and their endurance, toughness, and guts. I admire their skill and stuff, but the main thing is their heart.

Q: Have you seen Quintet, the post-apocalyptic science fiction movie directed by Robert Altman and starring Paul Newman? It shares similarities with The Salute of the Jugger, as both films revolve around a fictional post-holocaust game.

A: No, I remember hearing about it and hearing about the subject. And I just don't remember the movie. I think I'd already written Jugger at that time. But I'm not sure. So, I don't know. I just remember that it was there. And it had a similar subject. And I just don't remember if I ever saw it or not.

Q: Was directing the film always your aspiration?

A: It was a film I thought, possibly to direct, but I was more interested at that time in writing films. So, I just went on to the next one. Then I kept on writing and editing. I was still making a living as an editor in the late 70s. My first response was, I hadn't done the brilliant job as a director that I thought I was going to do. I'd had Tony Scott to be the director for a while. But we had some story disagreements, and Tony moved on to other things. And it would have been better if Tony Scott had directed because he's a class director, and I was a beginning director. So when it came out, it was not the job I'd intended to do, no fault of anybody but me. I had all the support I could want, a great producer, great cast, I had the budget, and if I did it after three more pictures, I would do it a lot better. I was a first-timer, and I think it shows in the picture. And that disappointed me. Another thing that disappointed me was that it was 10 years later than I wanted it to be. I'd written it in the late 70s. And that's when I wanted it to come out. At that time, when your makeup stuff would have been new to people. Not old and all of that stuff. So in both cases, Journey of the 14 Presidents, and The Salute of the Jugger were written back in the 70s, which is when things should have happened on those scripts. They would have been fresh and would have been a breakthrough kind of thing. And as it was, it was a little different from other pictures. I hadn't seen Terminator when I was writing Jugger. But later, seeing Terminator, what I loved about it was it raised the film above the genre. In other words, people who liked that genre would go see it. But people who didn't like that genre would go see it because it stepped up. I mean, it's just like when Rosemary's Baby and The Exorcist stepped up, and they weren't just run-of-the-mill horror films for a genre crowd. They were main things that grabbed all the audiences.

Q: Remembering Director Tony Scott

A: Tony Scott was an extraordinary director who has never been given the recognition he deserves because he was a really good director. He dealt with narrative better than his brother, and was fantastically exciting. I was a huge admirer of the original Taking of Pelham 123. I thought it was a wonderful film, beautifully directed, and Robert Shaw was in it. When Tony was going to remake it, I thought that was idiocy. You should never do that. It's too good of a film to be made as good again. But when I went to see it, with the exception of a couple of what I would call gratuitous car crashes, which I guess is what Tony's bread and butter is, it was fantastic. Beautifully written, beautifully acted. I'm not gonna say it's better than the first, but it's right up there with the first. It's beautiful and Denzel Washington is great and Travolta. As I said, it was a shock because I was prepared for, "Oh, my God, what a ridiculous thing to do." Sort of like somebody saying, "Well, I'm gonna remake Citizen Kane." But it was magnificent. He's a real, underappreciated director.

Q: Can you describe your experience of filming in Coober Pedy, Australia? This town has been in many films, including parts of Mad Max: Beyond Thunderdome.

A: Coober Pedy was used in Mad Max. Anyway, yeah, it was an amazing place. Absolutely amazing. And I'd never been there. And it's still a wonder to this day - I mean, people living underground and so on and so forth. The motel we lived in was partly underground, and the food had to come in weekly by a big truck. It was a real strange place and an adventure, and exciting. Also, most importantly, our second unit director, stunt coordinator, and actor, Guy Norris, worked on the Mad Max films. He was a very important part of Jugger.

Q: In the cast, you also had Hugh Keays Byrne, who was known for his role as the Toecutter in Mad Max. He was even in Fury Road as well.

A: I was not aware of that, curiously enough. I'm sure I'd seen him, but my memory of him is a wonderful performance he gave in Burke & Wills. It was directed by Graham Clifford and written by my good friend Michael Thomas. Hugh Keays Byrne was wonderful in it.

Q: The film captures the realistic portrayal of a post-apocalyptic wasteland, without CGI. It's all very realistic. Feels real.

A: Very. We didn't have the option of CGI in those days. Neither did Ridley Scott when he made Blade Runner. I do wish the Australian sky wasn't so postcard blue. Also, David Eggby did everything he could to tone it down, but it is an awful bright future.

Q: In terms of visuals, the film resembles the Mad Max series, particularly Beyond Thunderdome, in terms of its aesthetics and overall tone. Considering the involvement of cinematographer David Eggby, who had previously worked on the original 1979 Mad Max, and editor Richard Francis-Bruce, who also contributed to Mad Max: Beyond Thunderdome.

A: Richard Francis-Bruce, I didn't know he worked on Mad Max. He's a great editor. Well, the history of Mad Max, and my film, and I want to be very careful how I say this, because this could be a prickly subject for some people because I don't mean to offend anyone. But I wrote two dystopian screenplays in the late 70s. One was called The Salute of the Jugger, and the other was called Journey to the 14 Presidents. And that was a script about a bunch of guys hauling slaves in trucks across a wasteland and being hounded by guys on motorcycles who were like the Plains Indians, and they didn't have enough fuel or water or so on so forth. They even use the line in it when they're talking about the fuel as precious juice. And I wrote those scripts. And Journey to the 14 Presidents went off to Australia with some director whose name I forget now, can't remember his name, but it went to Australia. And then around 1980 or 81, I went to a screening of Mad Max, which was already a hit in Australia. Ridley was having the screening as he was working on Blade Runner. Tony and I were working on something called My Dogs on Fire, and we went to Ridley's screening and we saw Mad Max, which was quite wonderful. And I loved the business of the leg. And that was brilliant. And the film itself was very, very good. And it didn't seem to me, so close to anything I wrote, it was dystopian, and so on and so forth. And I thought it was very good, good narrative. But some years later, when I saw The Road Warrior, I was overwhelmed with how much of The Road Warrior seemed like Journey to the 14 Presidents. And it wasn't that anybody copied anything. In fact, George Miller's story, his narrative was much better than mine. And it was a beautifully done movie and I was very admiring of it. I thought, holy shit, he must have read Journey to the 14 Presidents. And years later when I saw Fury Road I thought, holy shit, this is even more like Journey to the 14 Presidents so I don't know if he ever read it but certainly had the impression that he was inspired by it, that's not a bad thing, when I wrote Soldier, I was very much inspired by Terminator. These things catch you, but I do think he must have read it. I may be wrong, and he can say he didn't. But I think he read it. Make no mistake, his story was his story and was very inventive and different. It was full of wonderful things that I never thought of, like the guy who had the plane. And that thing about the kid and from the kid's point of view, The Road Warrior is a great film.

I believe, in Journey to the 14 Presidents, which I haven't read for a long time, but I believe I described the motorcycle riders who were always attacking the truck convoy. I referred to them as like Plains Indians. So, they were like those Indians who rode on their ponies. And so fast and so gracefully and everything and attacked from horseback. And I wrote about the motorcyclists who I called ghosts, being like that. They were out there hunting the big trucks, and sort of like the Plains Indians hunted buffalo, but at any rate, I made some reference to that in there. And then when I saw Fury Road, I was literally seeing some of what I had written. I was very jealous, because that's how I envisioned those motorcyclists. He got that right.

Q: Charles Roven produced the film, and he has since gone on to do incredible work. You worked with him on Twelve Monkeys. What are your memories and working relationship with Chuck?

A: Well, for many years, he was a close friend. And he was a wonderful producer. He's the guy who helped me through The Salute of the Jugger and got it made. And he was a strong force. And later on, we worked with him again. But then we grew apart as he became bigger and more important, and we haven't talked to him in years. I miss him because he's a great producer and a wonderful person, but he's going on; he's got two pictures out this year. He's got Oppenheimer, and he's got Ferrari. And I remember him showing the Ferrari script something like 20 years ago. And talking about whether Jan and I wanted to rewrite it, and we could see it, and it was a script by Troy Kennedy Martin. We had rewritten another Troy Kennedy Martin script and ruined it. And lo and behold, he's got a solo screen credit on it, which is wonderful after all these years. So that's a wonderful thing. That Ferrari's coming out. I haven't seen it yet. But I look forward to it. He is a great producer.

Q: Rutger Hauer, who portrayed Sallow, was obviously quite a seasoned veteran of the sport in the film. Both of you have previously had a connection in Blade Runner, and you contributed to Ladyhawke. And he was an ideal fit for a role. Share your experience of working Rutger.

A: I did have a connection with Rutger, and he wrote the wonderful little coda to one of my speeches. He wrote the Tears in the Rain lines, which was beautiful. He brought that into the mix, so he was wonderful. However, I didn't know him well. I was hired to work on Ladyhawke almost immediately after Blade Runner. This was very early, long before Ladyhawke got made, and it came from a script by Ed Kamara. It was a good script, but I thought it was a schizophrenic script, with some parts being very friendly and lovely while others were dark. When Dick Donner and Lauren Shuler approached me about doing a rewrite, I said, "If you want the dark version, like a Kurosawa picture, then I'm your boy. But if you want the Disney version, get somebody else." So, I wrote a dark version that was pretty fucking dark. However, they weren't quite ready for that and brought in Michael Thomas. At that time, Blade Runner hadn't been released, and Rutger Hauer wasn't well-known. But I suggested Rutger Hauer to play this guy. Normally, I'm not good at casting, so they probably wrote me off and thought, "What do the writers know about casting?" which is fair enough. But some years later, after being rewritten by Michael Thomas, and then by that other guy, they did cast Rutger Hauer. The irony is, I wanted Rutger because he was such a dark guy, and I was writing a dark version of Ladyhawke. However, they didn't make the dark version but rather the light version. I don't think that was the best thing in the world, but he would have been great in the version that I wrote.

Rutger is a terrific actor right off. He's unbelievably good. He's very intense and very involved in his part, which is a good thing. I had some actors there who were really good, but they just walked through their parts without any of the intensity that Rutger puts into a role. Let me revise that, there were one or two, and it was my fault. In other words, I led them. I didn't understand acting at that time, and I was foolish. I didn't take advantage of their abilities by pushing them to go beyond a very thin portrayal. Rutger, on the other hand, I didn't push him on anything. He pushed me all the time. And he was very intense. One of the problems with Rutger, and this is interesting, was that he was a very bright man. He would come up with like 100 ideas in the morning. And I would be just swamped. As a first-time director, having 120 people working for me, Rutger giving me all these new ideas was overwhelming. The problem was that most of his ideas were just off the top of his head, and they were silly, not good ideas. But some of them were brilliant. I would be racking my brain trying to do my job and sort through all his ideas at the same time. He did have wonderful ideas, but you had to somehow wade through and get rid of all the stuff that he was just shooting off the top of his head. The absolute opposite of that was Joan Chen, who is a wonderful actor, but very measured and careful about what she says. Whenever she made a suggestion, it was absolutely right. I remember she pushed me to do something one time, and I thought, "Well, Joan's wrong. She doesn't know." But I shot it her way just because I respect her as an actress and want her to be happy. Later, when I saw it in the cutting room, I said to myself, "Oh, her way was right. What an idiot I am." I had a similar experience with a wonderful actress on Twelve Monkeys, Madeline Stowe. So, the same thing was true with Joan. And of course, Joan has gone on to be a very good director. I admire her tremendously. And by the way, for stories, if you're talking about The Salute of the Jugger. I think he was a fourth assistant director, the fourth AD, and we used him as an extra in that final scene that you see in The Salute of the Jugger. We call it Juggers of doom, and he's in that scene. He went on to be a super director in Australia. He directed Two Hands and Ned Kelly, and he turned out to be 100 times a better director than me. And I've always told other people, he learned everything from me. I'm sure that he rolls his eyes when he hears that because I was a first-time director who didn't know what the fuck he was doing. But at any rate, that's just an irony that that I'm sitting there being a director with the future director Gregor Jordan.

Q: Back to Joan Chen. She lends the role a blend of toughness and gravitas, which I think should be held in high regard, similar to Sigourney Weaver in Alien and Charlize Theron in Fury Road. What was your reaction to her performance and memories of working with her?

A: Fantastic, better than I could have imagined. Other good actors were competing for the role. And it was Chuck Roven who pushed her over the top. And he was right. She was fucking great and better than I could ever have imagined. And she's tough. And she's smart, and a pleasure to work with. So, she was just great.

Q: Did you always envision Kidda as an Asian woman?

A: I had originally envisioned her as an Asian woman. I originally saw her as Asian. I think I described her during the first draft as Asian because I was very multicultural. But when I started seeing actresses, my mind was open to anybody. So, I wasn't adamant that she had to be Asian. But Joan just won the part by being the best. I mean, she was great. She was very athletic and did as many of the stunts as she could, except for the back flips. But she did all those things on the hard cement floor. And she is tough. When Joan was preparing for the role, she didn't want to be an Asian princess. She was totally into the hardass part of it. She had previously played an

Asian princess, and that was fine. She did a good job, but now she wanted to be something completely different. She really impressed me. When you watch Salute of the Jugger and see Joan, you think of modern-day mixed martial arts and the women who fight in that sport. She was like them.

Q: What were your memories of working with Vincent D'Onofrio?

A: Well, Vince was an upcoming guy. And we've done some interviews. There's a documentary on the making of Jugger. I don't know if you've seen it. It was shot by Rutger's team, and he financed some camera crew or something. And we uncovered it a while ago, you know, these Australian guys are doing a documentary on Jugger and trying to get the picture remastered. And they came and did a bunch of interviews here and everything. And we dug up the old documentary that Rutger had done, so he had his camera person do an interview with Vince. Vince was saying, "Hey, this is my chance, you know, I'm going on to other things, but I'm young, and I'm in shape. And this is my only chance to do a part like this." He was very excited about it. But I think he did what actors often do. He read the script and thought the script was all about his character. When he actually got to making the movie, he realized he was one of many, and I think he was pretty disappointed. I think he thought he had made a mistake. But he did a great job. He was good and athletic and ready to do anything. He was terrific.

Q: Share your memories of the rest of cast?

A: Delroy Lindo was magnificent. And Anna Katrina was magnificent. Gandhi, for crying out loud, yes, great. And also, the guy who played Dog Boy, Justin Manchu, who's a successful writer in Australia, very good writer, the whole bunch of them. I was a lucky, lucky boy. I mean, I'm a first-time director out there in Australia, never worked with actors before, they could have killed me. But instead, they were supportive of me, helpful, and taught me so much. I had not understood what actors did till I got there. And all of them were patient with me. And it's scary to be an actor out there, in Australia, with a first-time director, and yet they sucked it up. They didn't display their fear. And they helped me through the picture. And I'm forever indebted to them. And they gave good performances. There's no way to talk about the actors in Jugger without mentioning Max Fairchild. Holy smokes, he gave a wonderful performance. He's a fantastic actor and he became a friend of mine. So I just want to make sure that when I talk about the actors, I'm also talking about Max. What an actor!

Q: How about the music score for the film?

A: Todd Boekelheide is a great composer, and I'm just astonished that he didn't get big offers from the movie industry. However, he has Academy Awards as a mixer and used to work at Skywalker Ranch, which is the Lucas place. He is a great composer, and I have heard blatant rip-offs of his Jugger music in other movies. His music has been copied, especially the opening music. I am in awe of him. On one hand, I am ashamed that I made him write something that he thought was unmusical, but it helped the film more. It's like when you are writing a picture and they make you write something lousy, but it makes the picture better [laughs]. I felt, Jesus, now I'm in the role of taking an artist and making him do something he is uncomfortable with. It was just one little part, but throughout the whole movie, he proves to be an exceptional composer who deserves more recognition. He has had great success, especially in the documentary world and in low budget features. He is absolutely fantastic.

Q: The costume design by Terry Ryan and the art department memories.

A: Oh my God, those guys were good. You know, I have the pictures, their artwork. I kept photos of them so they come up on my screensaver. But John Stoddard and his whole crew, Terry Ryan and John, his art department. Whoa, you should see the sketches they drew. Their great art and then of course, what they put on the screen and the way they made the Red City work. I mean, those guys were amazing, to have them with no budget, they did it with no budget. So I mean, these guys were just plain breathtakingly good. John Stoddard was a friend. I've lost touch with him since I became a grandfather because I'd become a different person, but he was a wonderful friend as well as a superb production designer.

Q: The Makeup team memories.

A: The makeup is great. Bob McCarran, he was a wonderful human being. Yeah, Bob McCarran. He was a good man. He came in and did this stuff. But he said, "Hey, a Komodo dragon, I could make a cast of it, right?" We got ourselves a Komodo dragon. I couldn't believe it. These guys were all artists, and I was just privileged to be in that company. And if I could ever learn how to manage stuff, I would love to be a director just to work with people like that. Unfortunately, I'm not a good manager. I don't know how to do that. And so that was my big weakness. I was very fortunate that everybody was helpful and kind, Chuck Roven supported me, and the actors supported me, and everybody got me through it. And I wish I thought like a director and was a talented director. I have increased respect for all my directors. God bless them, Clint Eastwood, Stephen Frears, Terry Gilliam, all these guys. What they do is just beyond my belief.

Q: Everyone is influenced in some way or another. James Cameron has even cited Mad Max as an influence on him for The Terminator. If you watch the original Mad Max film, after Max gets

shot in the leg, he develops a severe limp. There is a shot from a low angle from behind, showing him dragging his leg as he makes his way back to his car. Cameron used a similar low-angle shot from behind in The Terminator film when the Terminator is hit by a semi-truck (similar to Toecutter's death). The Terminator walks from the back of the truck towards the cabin, dragging his leg like Max did. It is a form of flattery, if anything.

A: It's good for Cameron to acknowledge his debt to The Terminator.

Q: With The Salute of the Jugger, like the Mad Max films, your film has profoundly impacted global culture. It also served as a source for developing the game of jugger. When did you hear about your game, The Jugger, being played for real, and what was your response?

A: One of the first times I heard about it was from a friend of ours, who had gone off to be a DEA agent, or maybe he was working for prosecuting attorneys or something in Las Vegas; or something. He called us from Vegas to say that he had passed a group of people playing Jugger. I was quite astonished. I think this must have been in '91 or something like that. Anyway, he called and said, "Hey, they're playing your game." I thought that was thrilling. I had always wanted it to be a cult movie. It's sort of a culty thing for them to be playing the game. Gradually, I heard more and more about it, and then I knew some people who played the game. We had a relationship, some sort of relationship, and we became friends and so on. So I loved the game. The idea that people were playing it because it meant they were watching the movie. I liked that even more than playing the game.

Q: David Twohy, co-writer of Waterworld, has acknowledged Mad Max 2 as a significant influence on the movie. Both films

were lensed by cinematographer Dean Semler. Were you involved in any uncredited screenwriting for Waterworld?

A: Absolutely not. The only thing that's true about it is that I was asked by both a universal executive and by Kevin Costner to come in and Kevin Reynolds was a guy I knew and was friendly with. I was asked to do a rewrite, but I was busy working on Twelve Monkeys. And I did not want to take a break from the other script. So I didn't want to work on Waterworld, but I also didn't know what I would do that would help it. So I had nothing whatsoever to do with Waterworld, apart from turning down a rewrite.

Q: Waterworld, that's another one that's post-apocalyptic.

A: Absolutely. It's very [laughs], what's the word, dystopian? Yes, it was very good. And I liked the world. And I liked the ideas and stuff.

Q: If I'm right, you and Janet Peoples were also inspired by the Book of Revelations.

A: Yes, well, we liked the Book of Revelations. And we tried to include as much of it in Twelve Monkeys as possible without making the film solely about the Bible or something. The Book of Revelations was an important part of Twelve Monkeys. And we screwed it up. Because when we had the guy take the vials of the virus and everything, we forgot to include the correct number of cities, because, as you may remember, the Book of Revelations mentions seven vials. And we should have had seven cities, but we didn't. So, in any case, we made a little mistake there. But we were trying to suggest that the Book of Revelations had been written by scientists from the future, searching for the past. And we had fun playing with that idea. Terry Gilliam is the kind of guy who does those kinds of things because he has an eye for the absurd like nobody else, and he loves absurdity and things like that. So, it was fun. It was good.

Q: The Salute of the Jugger initially failed upon its release.

A: It was a bomb. The Salute of the Jugger, the bottom line is that it was the original movie. And then for American audiences, it was called The Blood of Heroes. I cut it down at the request of the financier, the guy who ran Kings Road. And the thing is, I didn't want to cut it. If you have screenings and stuff like that, and the audience doesn't enthuse about your picture, you're very vulnerable. And it's very hard to argue how terrific your picture is, if the audience doesn't think so. I couldn't argue. I mean, I thought, well, maybe this will help the film and be better and so on. So I cut it back as he requested. Or pretty much as he requested and released it again, and still didn't do business. So what the hell.

Q: Through the passage of time, how do you perceive the film, after all this time?

A: If people like it, I'm happy. I love it when people like the movie. I mean, I feel that way about anything I work on. If people like it, I'm so happy because that's what I'm intending. I'm not some great artist or someone who's sitting there working on obscure works of genius. I want to entertain people. And when the movie fails to entertain people, I'm broken-hearted. So anything that gives people enjoyment from the movie is good with me.

Q: Would you like to have directed more pictures?

A: I did try to direct another film, and it didn't work out for reasons. But basically, I'm not a director. I don't think like a director. I don't have a director's mindset. It's not my strength. And I found it terrifying to be a director. I'm much better at writing, and I'm comfortable with that. I mean, I can't be comfortable doing hard work, so I'm not comfortable writing. But I know what I'm doing. When I'm a writer, I'm much better than I would ever be as a director. And to be a director, you have to think like one, and I don't.

The Salute of the Jugger – The Sport of Jugging

Jugging can have two distinct meanings: one of the most popular games is known as "Jugger" and in some parts of the world, this term is used to refer to hunting or poaching. Both meanings below:

Jugger (Sport): Jugger is the team game that also started in Germany and got the ideas from the 1989 movie "The Salute of the Jugger" also known as "The Blood of Heroes." That's a game that is played with a ball and a set of padded sticks with foam on the end. The game looks like some mix of rugby and fencing in which two teams battle for points counting when the ball (or "skull") lands in the opponent's goal. Each team is made up of players filling certain roles, like runners, defenders and one person called "the Qwik" that can run with the ball and score. Jugger has become a popular sport in the world, and the organised events include leagues and tournaments for the fans of this sport.

Jugging (Hunting/Poaching): In some localities, 'jugging' may include 'trapping' or 'poaching' of wild animals whereby traps are set and cunning methods are used to kill and capture the wild animals. On the other hand, it is significant to recognize that trophy hunting is a frequently misused term, being extensively associated with illegal or immoral hunting practices that are carried out using techniques that are banned by law.

The use of the word "Jugging" could be taken in many ways, whether it refers to the coding of characters in the Jugger game or refers to traditional hunting practices. Jugger as a sport is massively cultivated among students of German colleges and universities across the world. They have gained so much popularity that there is even a national league. There are Australian teams, New Zealander teams, Austrian teams, Irish teams, English teams, Polish teams, Czech teams, Denmark teams, Spanish teams, Sweden teams, Colombian teams, Costa Rican teams, Dutch teams, Latvian teams, Lithuanian teams, Canadian, Mexican and Roman as well.[109]

There are many different versions of the game with different rules and objectives as well.[110] Some focus on teamwork, speed, and skillfulness; these are called "sports jugger." However, there are games that look very similar to the exciting and visually striking sport shown in the film, frequently referred to as "wasteland jugger."

The first worldwide tournament for the sport jugger was held in Hamburg, Germany on May 20th of 2007. Teams from Northern Germany and the Irish team named Setanta participated in this event. Next year, Australia and Ireland went to Germany after the initial German Open. It was the first jugger tournament with teams from two different continents. The World Club Championships happen every two years biennially and they bring together players from four continents - Europe, Australia, North America, and South America.

The aim of the game is to get the ball, called "skull," from the middle of the field and put it into the other team's goal, named "mal" or "mound." There are five players in each team but just one can touch and hold the ball. This player has the name "quick" or is also known as a runner. The other four players, who people call enforcers or pumpers, have swords with padding or a foam ball that is tied to a string. They have the job of making room for their runner to get to the target by touching players on the other team. The runners can participate in wrestling, much like what is observed in rugby.[111]

The thing people often call "skull" in the German language has various names that change with the region's traditions.[112] In Ber-

---

[109]   *"The International Jugger Council". juggercouncil.org.*

[110]   *"Jugger Rulebooks Archive of all known Jugger rules". www.juggerblog.net.*

[111]   *Jugger EXPLAINED in 45 seconds - what is Jugger? https://youtu.be/H5KGov_Sajs?si=ECRFUD2l8leo-vyB*

[112]   *On the two traditions see also: Jugger. A post-apocalyptic sport for all occasions, Morrisville 2008, pp. 18–20*

lin, they say 'Jugg' for it, but in the Hamburg or Dilettanten area, they use 'Schädel' to name it. In these customs, the skull they use is basically a sphere shaped to look like a dog's head. The skulls for these props are often created from foam and tape, which is different from how in "The Blood of Heroes/The Salute of the Jugger" real dog skulls were utilized. Foam and tape are used for making it last longer. In countries like Germany and Ireland, people often use a dog skull that is created from cell foam with a latex covering for such needs.

Saluting Rutger Hauer
(23 January 1944 – 19 July 2019)

Recording of the Youth Series Floris by the NTS at Doornenburg Castle in the Betuwe. The title role Floris van Rosemondt is played by Rutger Hauer September 19, 1968.[53]Eric Koch for Anefo - NationaalArchief.

Film adaptation of Turkish Delight (based on the 1969 novel by Jan Wolkers) by Paul Verhoeven. Lead actors Rutger Hauer and Monique van de Ven June 7, 1972.[54] Rob Mieremet / Anefo - NationaalArchief.

Collection / Archive: Photo collection Anefo Report / Series: Film adaptation of Turkish Delight (based on the 1969 novel by Jan Wolkers) by Paul Verhoeven Description: Actors Rutger Hauer and Monique van de Ven Keywords: actors, film, group portrait Copyright holder: National Archives Material type: Negative (black/white) Archive inventory number: view access 2.24.01.05 Component number: 925-6530.[55]

Photo about a movie directed by Paul Verhoeven based on Turks Fruit from 1969 which was written by Jan Wolkers. From left to right: actor Rutger Hauer, writer Jan Wolkers and actress Monique van de Ven.[56]FotograafOnbekend / Anefo.

Collection / Archive: Photo collection Anefo Report / Series : The premiere of the film "Soldaat van Oranje" is attended by the royal family Description : Rutger Hauer (left) and Jeroen Krabbé on motorcycle upon arrival Date : September 21, 1977 Location : Amsterdam, North Holland.[113] Photographer: Verhoeff, Bert / Anefo.

Film recording Grijpstra and the Vulture A'dam, 1979.[57]Fotopersbureau De Boer - FilmopnameGrijpstraen de Gier A'dam, Noord-Hollands Archief.

---

[113]   *By Bert Verhoeff / Anefo - http://proxy.handle.net/10648/aca314d4-d0b4-102d-bcf8-003048976d84,   CC0,   https://commons.wikimedia.org/w/index.php?cu-rid=65702511*

Rutger Hauer, who was a notable actor from the Netherlands, came into this world on January 23 of 1944 in Breukelen. He passed away sadly on July 19 in the year of 2019 but he is remembered for his remarkable acting work. Hauer was recognized for his unique look, with sharp blue eyes, and his strong acting skills. He worked together six times with famous director Paul Verhoeven on projects including the TV series "Floris" in 1969, and films like "Turkish Delight" from 1973, "Keetje Tippel" in 1975, "Soldier of Orange" from 1977, "Spetters" made in 1980, and "Flesh+Blood" released during 1985.

Hauer became famous all over the world for playing Roy Batty—a bad android, in Ridley Scott's science fiction movie "Blade Runner" (1982). His portrayal of this deep-thinking character is one of his best-known roles. The "Tears in Rain" speech by Hauer is seen as one of the most unforgettable moments ever on film.

Rutger Hauer, in his professional acting life, acted in many different types of movies. He played important parts like the titular character in "The Hitcher" from 1986, where he was a scary and mysterious person who hitchhikes. Also, he was Etienne Navarre in "Ladyhawke," made by Richard Donner in 1985; it's a love story with actors Matthew Broderick and Michelle Pfeiffer. He acted in "Blind Fury" from the year 1989 and also was in "The Legend of the Holy Drinker," a film made in 1988, along with many more.

Rutger Hauer had a long career in acting that lasted for many years, and his roles have left a strong impression on film lovers and people who watch movies. People recognized him for being able to play many different kinds of roles very well, having an engaging way of appearing in films, and playing characters that were complicated and stayed with you long after watching them.

Critical Reviews of Blade Runner

Howard Waldstein, CBR.com: "Rutger Hauer's "tears in the rain" monologue is just about the greatest science-fiction monologue to ever exist."[114]

Roger Ebert, *Chicago Sun-Times*: "This is a seminal film, building on older classics like Metropolis or Things to Come, but establishing a pervasive view of the future that has influenced science fiction films ever since."[115]

Shawn Levy, *The Oregonian*: "'I've seen things you people wouldn't believe,' declares one of the androids late in the going. And if you've seen this film, you can make the same claim."[116]

Sara Michelle Fetters, MovieFreak.com: "Its melding of Raymond Chandler gumshoe noir with Dick's trademark dour cybernetic musings is borderline magnificent, the themes of alienation and identity so inherent in the novel nearly popping right off the screen."[117]

Critical Reviews of Ladyhawke

Sheila Benson, *Los Angeles Times*: "The actors are extravagantly good: Hauer, as always, with a sense of intelligence behind his physical exploits; Pfeiffer, strong and exquisite, and Broderick, embroidering on his role as go-between, is irresistible, comic and wistful by turns."[118]

Ian Nathan, Empire: "Here is the kind of elaborate, gothic tragedy that fuels Germanic operas and Heavy Metal ballads — the lovers who can remain together but forever be apart."[119]

---

[114] *Howard Waldstein, CBR.com https://www.cbr.com/10-best-sci-fi-films-of-the-80s-ranked/#starman-1984*

[115] *Roger Ebert, Chicago Sun Times (November 9, 2007).*

[116] *Shawn Levy, Oregonian (October 26, 2007).*

[117] *Sara Michelle Fetters, MovieFreak.com*

[118] *MOVIE REVIEWS: MEDIEVAL MAGIC, MODERN ROMP: 'Ladyhawke'https://www.latimes.com/archives/la-xpm-1985-04-12-ca-8024-story.html*

[119] *https://www.empireonline.com/movies/reviews/ladyhawke-review/*

Keith Phipps, The Dissolve: "It's a likable-enough adventure that feels much smaller than the widescreen landscapes in which it takes place."[120]

Matthew Turner, Hero Collector: "A thoroughly delightful fantasy romance that holds up remarkably well and deserves to be rediscovered by today's younger audiences."[121]

Critical Reviews of Flesh & Blood

Dragan Antulov, rec.arts.movies.reviews: "One of the most under-rated gems of 1980s."[122]

Nicholas Bell, IONCINEMA.com: "An examination of medieval Europe that attempts to correctly reconcile romantic notions with exaggerated realism, Flesh+Blood is a lost mid-80's classic from an underrated and challenging auteur."[123]

J.R. Southall, Starburst: "Flesh+Blood hasn't lost any of its gruesome power."[124]

Fernando F. Croce, CinePassion: "Religion and marriage and the very idea of heroism are hurled into Verhoeven's bestial pyre, his direction has the gift of overabundance – the Spanish locations and castles teem with putrid lushness."[125]

Critical Reviews of The Hitcher

Chuck O'Leary, FulvueDrive-in.com: "Rutger Hauer is so menacing as the title fiend that you'll never pick up a hitchhiker. An absolutely relentless horror-thriller."[126]

---

[120]   *https://thedissolve.com/reviews/1619-ladyhawke/*

[121]   *Matthew Turner, Hero Collector (Jul 9, 2021).*

[122]   *Dragan Antulovrec.arts.movies.reviews (January 1, 2000).*

[123]   *Nicholas Bell IONCINEMA.com (September 23, 2014).*

[124]   *https://www.starburstmagazine.com/reviews/fleshblood-1985/*

[125]   *https://www.cinepassion.org/Reviews/f/FleshBlood.html*

[126]   *Chuck O'Leary, FulvueDrive-in.com (October 10, 2005).*

Widgett Walls, Needcoffee.com: "It's like a sadistic version of Duel, instead of a semi you get Hauer in all his creepy manic splendor."[127]

Tim Brayton Antagony & Ecstasy: "A cosmic horror film drawn out of a psychological thriller."[128]

Fred Topel, About.com: "Effective '80s horror movie. A relentless villain and some horrific scenes."[129]

Critical Reviews of Blind Fury

Felix Vasquez Jr., Cinema Crazed: "A satisfying action vehicle for Hauer..."[130]

Caffeinated Clint, Moviehole: "One of Hauer's best flicks."[131]

Scott Weinberge, FilmCritic.com: "Solid B-level actioner with lots of mayhem and the great Rutger Hauer."[132]

Matt Brunson, Film Frenzy: "This did provide Rutger Hauer with perhaps his most unusual heroic role until Hobo with a Shotgun 22 years later."[133]

Critical Reviews of Hobo with a Shotgun

Jim Schembri, The Age (Australia): "Gloriously over-the-top blood pudding about a homeless man (Hauer) who goes Dirty Harry on a dead-end town run by sadistic crims."[134]

---

[127] *Widgett Walls Needcoffee.com (March 19, 2003)*

[128] *https://www.alternateending.com/2014/08/summer-of-blood-slasher-adjacent-films.html*

[129] *Fred Topel About.com (Jul 14, 2003).*

[130] *https://www.cinema-crazed.com/blog/2012/08/22/blind-fury-1989/*

[131] *Caffeinated Clint, Moviehole (May 6, 2005).*

[132] *Scott Weinberg eFilmCritic.com (July 26, 2002).*

[133] *https://thefilmfrenzy.com/2021/01/15/view-from-the-couch-love-and-monsters-silent-running-etc/*

[134] *https://www.theage.com.au/entertainment/movies/hobo-with-a-shotgun-review-20110721-1hqds.html*

Anna Smith, metro.co.uk: "Hobo with a Shotgun is as likely to please Quentin Tarantino fans as it is to offend everyone else, with scenes of elaborate decapitations and scantily clad women writhing in the ensuing blood spatter."[135]

Victoria Alexander, FilmsInReview.com: "It's a grindhouse mess but it stars Rutger Hauer!"[136]

Kim Newman, *Empire* magazine: "Hauer's best since The Hitcher. If Eisener calms down, he may have a career outside live-action 'toons."[137]

---

[135]   *https://metro.co.uk/2011/07/14/hobo-with-a-shotgun-rutger-hauer-film-review-77454/*

[136]   *https://filmfestivaltoday.com/film-reviews/film-review-hobo-with-a-shotgun*

[137]   *Kim Newman, Empire Magazine (July 11, 2011).*

Saluting Hugh Keays-Byrne
(18 May 1947 – 1 December 2020)

Hugh Keays-Byrne, a famous actor from England and Australia, had his birthday on May 18 in the year 1947. Sadly, he left us on December 1 in the year 2020. Keays-Byrne gained impressive popularity due to his outstanding performances in two well-known Australian movies about a world after the apocalypse: "Mad Max" (1979) and "Mad Max: Fury Road" (2015).

In the first "Mad Max" movie, Keays-Byrne played Toecutter, who is the scary boss of a very tough bike rider gang. After many years, he returned to play another bad guy named Immortan Joe in "Mad Max: Fury Road."

Beyond his remarkable participation in the "Mad Max" films, Hugh Keays-Byrne experienced a broad acting career that covered movies and television. He embarked on an accomplished journey in the showbiz industry, both inside Australia and around the world. He received much praise and was recognized by loyal fans of the "Mad Max" series for his remarkable work in it.

Critical Reviews of Mad Max

Kathy Fennessy, Seattle Film Blog: "As a filmmaker, George Miller keeps cliche at bay through his attention to detail even as he hews to revenge-thriller archetype..."[138]

Stephen Danay, Under the Radar: "Mad Max is a straight forward fusion of two B-movie genres popular in the 1970s: the car chase film and the vigilante revenge film."[139]

---

[138] *https://siffblog2.blogspot.com/2022/02/mad-max-kl-studio-classics-australia.html*

[139] *https://www.undertheradarmag.com/reviews/mad_max_collectors_edition/*

Rob Gonsalves, Rob's Movie Vault: "George Miller's influential, hyperkinetic debut."[140]

Bruce McCabe, *Boston Globe*: "If punk is a sensibility as well as an adjective, Mad Max is a punk movie. Its Australian setting enhances it, authenticating its futuristic aura."[141]

Critical Reviews of Mad Max: Fury Road

Jennifer Bisset, CNET: "The entire movie takes place over one absolutely bonkers chase sequence. Its cinematic stats are jaw-dropping..."[142]

Sarah Marshall, Bitch Media: "Mad Max: Fury Road is a movie with the kind of reach most people - and even most movies - can only aspire to."[143]

Tony Asankomah, GhMovieFreak: "Although it's cold, violent and visceral you can also feel the underlying elements of hope, loyalty, reverence and redemption."[144]

Chris McCoy, *Memphis Flyer*: "It's a rare film that engages the mind while rocking the body. Miller's vision of a world consumed by its own greed, where water, gasoline, and bullets are the most precious commodities, seems even more relevant today than it did 30 years ago."[145]

---

[140] *https://letterboxd.com/martinblank/film/mad-max/*

[141] *Bruce McCabe Boston Globe (April 27, 2018)*

[142] *https://www.cnet.com/culture/entertainment/the-30-best-films-of-the-decade-ranked/*

[143] *https://www.bitchmedia.org/post/mad-max-complicates-action-hero-masculinity%E2%80%94and-thats-great*

[144] *https://ghmoviefreak.com/movie-review-mad-max-fury-road-2015-madness-to-redemption/*

[145] *https://www.memphisflyer.com/mad-max-fury-road?oid=3906374*

Saluting Max Fairchild
(22 August 1946 – 12 October 2017)

Max Fairchild, who is from Australia and worked as an actor, has become known for his acting in movies and on TV. He has been important to the film industry in Australia for many years. Fairchild is recognized for playing different characters, like Benno in "Mad Max" (1979) and a role in "Stone" (1974). He also acted on TV shows and more movies, adding variety to the Australian entertainment scene.

Saluting Joan Chen

Joan Chen, who was born in Shanghai, China on the 26th of April, 1961, is an actress with Chinese and American backgrounds. She also directs films, writes screenplays and produces movies. Her work is recognized in both China's film industry and Hollywood.

Chen started working in China as an actress and was seen in important movies like "Little Flower" from 1979 and "Xiu Xiu: The Sent-Down Girl" which came out in 1998. When she acted in the second one, many people praised her work very much, and she became known around the world. This happened while Chen Kaige, who is a famous movie director, was directing her.

In the US, Chen became known for playing Josie Packard in "Twin Peaks" (1990-1991), a quirky yet popular TV show produced by David Lynch. People really liked her acting as this mysterious and complicated person, which brought her many devoted fans.

Chen has acted in films from America, for example "The Last Emperor" from 1987 made by Bernardo Bertolucci, and Oliver Stone's film "Heaven & Earth" from 1993. Her work went on in movies across the Pacific Ocean, with roles in "Saving Face" of 2004 and a movie named "The Home Song Stories," which came out in 2007.

Joan Chen has directed and produced movies, too. She first directed the film "Xiu Xiu: The Sent-Down Girl" in 1998, a movie she also co-wrote. Besides this, she has directed television series episodes like "Halt and Catch Fire" and "Awake."

Her work has shown she is very adaptable and skilled in the movie industries of China and America, gaining her a significant place within the entertainment field.

Actor Joan Chen in costume as Marilyn Monroe in Dim Sum: A Little Bit of Heart in 1983. Photograph by Nancy Wong.[58]

Actor Joan Chen, in a deleted scene from Wayne Wang's Dim Sum: A Little Bit of Heart as she sings "My Boyfriend's Back (song)" in Cantonese on location in the Empress of China Restaurant on Grant Avenue in San Francisco, California. Many of the deleted scenes went into the making of "Dim Sum Take Out." Photograph by Nancy Wong San Francisco, California 1983.[59]

Saluting Delroy Lindo

Delroy Lindo, who is an actor from both Britain and America, came into the world on November 18, 1952 in Eltham, which is a part of London in England. He has built up a successful career across movies, TV shows and stage plays and people know him well because he can play many different kinds of roles. In his large collection of roles, Lindo has portrayed many unforgettable characters. His important movie work includes outstanding acting in films like "Malcolm X" from 1992, "Crooklyn" from 1994, "Clockers" and "Get Shorty," both released in 1995, as well as the film called "The Cider House Rules" that came out in 1999. He has also influenced television by contributing to series like "The Chicago Code" and "The Good Fight."

Critical Reviews of Malcolm X

Lynden Barber, *Sydney Morning Herald*: "Unusually rich, absorbing and often brilliant film-making, an epic deserving of the description. But that doesn't stop it from being worryingly ambiguous."[146]

Brian Susbielles, InSession Film: "Only a director like Lee could have produced this saga and feature a strong supporting cast with Delroy Lindo, Angela Bassett, Albert Hall, and a slew of cameos."[147]

Aaron Neuwirth, Why So Blu: "I look at Malcolm X as being one of the most important films not to be nominated for Best Picture. Of course, that hasn't stopped its legacy from building over time."[148]

Scott G. Mignola, Common Sense Media: "Insightful and well-rounded portrait of Malcolm X."[149]

---

[146] *The Sydney Morning Herald, Page 29 (March 4, 1993).*

[147] *https://insessionfilm.com/criterion-releases-november-2022/*

[148] *https://whysoblu.com/malcolm-x-the-criterion-collection-4k-uhd-blu-ray-review/*

[149] *https://www.commonsensemedia.org/movie-reviews/malcolm-x*

Critical Reviews of Crooklyn

Emanuel Levy, EmanuelLevy.Com: "Loosely based on Spike Lee's growing up in Brooklyn in the 1970s, the casual, warm, apolitical (for Lee) script took a life of its own during the development process."[150]

Saffron Maeve, Screen Slate: "An elegiac Bed-Stuy fairy tale."[151]

Anderson Jones, *Detroit Free Press*: "Because Lee's previous films have been so fervently about something that they smothered much of the very humanity Crooklyn celebrates, the relaxed gait is strikingly apparent."[152]

Critical Reviews of Clockers

Margaret A. McGurk, *Cincinnati Enquirer*: "Clockers is a tremendous film – and a major addition to the work of a vibrantly talented director."[153]

Sean Burns, WBUR's Arts & Culture: "Spike Lee's most sorrowful film. It's a devastating depiction of a community poisoning itself."[154]

Steve Persall, *Tampa Bay Times*: "Strong performances, edgy dialogue and Lee's success in luring an audience into his own tempo and urgent perspective make Clockers tough stuff, indeed."[155]

Critical Reviews of Get Shorty

David Ansen, *Newsweek*: "Hollywood has been in love with mobsters since the beginning of movies. But the other side of the equation has seldom been considered. That is, until now."[156]

---

[150]   *Emanuel Levy EmanuelLevy.Com (June 6, 2006).*

[151]   *https://www.screenslate.com/articles/crooklyn*

[152]   *Detroit Free Press, Page 32. (May 13, 1994).*

[153]   *The Cincinnati Enquirer, Page 28 (September 13, 1995).*

[154]   *https://www.wbur.org/news/2023/08/19/the-coolidge-corner-theatre-50-years-hip-hop-film-series*

[155]   *https://www.tampabay.com/archive/1995/09/13/spike-lee-makes-clockers-tick/*

[156]   *David Ansen, Newsweek (May 7, 2008).*

Dennis Schwartz, Movie Reviews: "A pleasing satire on gangsters, hustlers and Hollywood."[157]

Michael Dequina, TheMovieReport.com: "Has more than a few nasty quips directed at Hollywood and the vacuous, egotistical people who populate it."[158]

Jonathan Rosenbaum, *Chicago Reader*: "An entertaining comedy-thriller adapted by Scott Frank from the Elmore Leonard bestseller and directed with bounce (if not much nuance) by Barry Sonnenfeld."[159]

Critical Reviews of The Cider House Rules

Bob Graham, *San Francisco Chronicle*: "[It] is a fable that turns into a 1940s New England variation on Charles Dickens. It is also one dickens of an American movie."[160]

John R. McEwen, Film Quips Online: "It blends romance with the love of children, the warmth of family with the darker side of human nature, and the all-encompassing belief that everything has a purpose."[161]

Robin Clifford, Reeling Reviews: "There's quality here and that's a real good thing."[162]

Ron Wells, Film Threat: "What the film is really about are CHOICES: the need to make them, how they affect others, and actively dealing with the repercussions of your actions."[163]

---

[157]   *https://dennisschwartzreviews.com/getshorty/*

[158]   *https://themoviereport.com/movierpt1.html#getshorty*

[159]   *https://chicagoreader.com/movies/capsules/13072_GET_SHORTY*

[160]   *https://www.sfgate.com/movies/article/Dickens-Spirit-Guides-Cider-House-Tobey-2889903.php*

[161]   *http://www.filmquipsonline.com/ciderhouserules.html*

[162]   *https://www.reelingreviews.com/reel/219/#theciderhouserules*

[163]   *Ron Wells, Film Threat, (Dec 8, 2002).*

Saluting Vincent D'Onofrio

Vincent D'Onofrio, a renowned American actor and producer, has attained remarkable success throughout his extensive career. He is widely lauded for delivering outstanding performances in a variety of movies and TV series. Among his notable portrayals are Pvt. Leonard Lawrence "Gomer Pyle" in the 1987 film "Full Metal Jacket," Edgar the Bug in the 1997 film "Men in Black," and Wilson Fisk in the Netflix series "Daredevil" from 2015 to 2018. These examples are a testament to his exceptional talent and impressive body of work.

Critical Reviews of Full Metal Jacket

Jay Scott, *Globe and Mail*: "Full Metal Jacket is violent, caustic, ironic, and cold, an amoral object formed from a camera gliding majestically across slow-motion carnage while refusing to blink an eye or shed a tear."[164]

Henry Sheehan, *Chicago Reader*: "The most horrifying moments of Full Metal Jacket are those in which the young Americans gladly assist in their own damnation."[165]

Ed Travis, Hollywood Jesus: "Full Metal Jacket is a master study in indoctrination and fundamental identity shifts. Every moment of the film builds and builds on Kubrick's ideas..."[166]

Andrew Pollard, Starburst: "A hard-hitting movie laced with moments of dark humour and brimming with social commentary, Full Metal Jacket is viewed as one of the all-time great war movies."[167]

---

[164] *Jay Scott Globe and Mail (December 7, 2022).*

[165] *https://chicagoreader.com/film/marine-monsters/*

[166] *https://hollywoodjesus.com/full-metal-jacket/*

[167] *https://www.starburstmagazine.com/reviews/full-metal-jacket-4k-uhd/*

Critical Reviews of Men In Black

Stephen Thompson, AV Club: "Men in Black deserves credit for supplementing its special effects with a breezy script and genuinely charismatic performances by Will Smith and Tommy Lee Jones."[168]

Gene Siskel, *Chicago Tribune*: "A smart, funny and hip adventure film in a summer of car wrecks and explosions."[169]

Todd McCarthy, *Variety*: "A wild knuckleball of a movie that keeps dancing in and out of the strike zone."[170]

Peter Travers, *Rolling Stone*: "Director Barry Sonnenfeld loads the bases with action, fantasy and laughs, and hits a grand slam."[171]

---

[168] *https://www.avclub.com/men-in-black-1798195278*

[169] *https://articles.chicagotribune.com/1997-07-04/entertainment/9707040101_1_ alien-wild-america-black*

[170] *https://variety.com/1997/film/reviews/men-in-black-1117432622/*

[171] *https://www.rollingstone.com/tv-movies/tv-movie-reviews/men-in-black-115500/*

Cult-Movie Review: Rollerball (1975)

(By John Kenneth Muir Copyright © John Kenneth Muir)

"Corporate society takes care of everything. And all it asks of anyone, all it's ever asked of anyone ever, is not to interfere with management decisions."

- Corporate Executive, Bartholomew (John Houseman) explains how it is in Norman Jewison's Rollerball (1975)

Released the same year as the low-budget "Death Race 2000" (1975), director Norman Jewison's "Rollerball" is a dystopian film with many similar elements. Both films are set in the future. Both films involve "athletes" in incredibly dangerous contests, and both efforts suggest the notion of such violent contests as "bread and circuses" for the unhappy masses of America.

When the chips are down, give us our gladiatorial games, and we'll forget that we don't have our liberty...

Of course, "Death Race 2000" is more over-the-top, funny, and nasty in execution, and so "Rollerball" feels a bit reserved and staid by comparison. And yet "Rollerball" is grave, impressive, and serious in its depiction of a corporate dystopia. The film thrives on speed, acceleration and movement, and James Caan is a sturdy anchor in this tale of a world in which corporations use blood lust to control the people.

Not all critics agreed. Writing in *The Film Encyclopedia*, Science Fiction (page 327), a reviewer complained the film was "overly complicated" and mixed "political intrigue and romance for no purpose."

Others felt the film was just a cover for violence itself. Writing in *Sci-Fi Now* (Octopus Books, 1977), author Alan Frank noted that the film merely created a "special environment in which the film's excessive use of violence can be made justified."

By pointed contrast, recent assessments of "Rollerball" have been more positive. Film Threat noted that "Rollerball" was "prescient about violence, corporations, and TV," and that's certainly a fair assessment. The film is a valuable one because it questions what passes for entertainment, but more than that, what passes for "freedom" in an increasingly technological, media-saturated age.

"Ladies and gentlemen, will you stand please for the playing of our Corporate Hymn?"

"Rollerball"'s action takes place after the world's nations have gone "bankrupt," and after the destructive "Corporate Wars" have come and gone

Now, corporations "take care of everyone," and the violent, team sport of Rollerball has been created by big business to remind people of "the futility of individual effort." The goal of the corporations is to be essential to every individual's life, and for "the few" to make important decisions on "a global basis."

Unfortunately, there are serious downsides to corporate rule as depicted in "Rollerball." For one thing, all citizens are treated as powerless employees of the "Executive Class." This means that your beloved wife can be transferred to another man's possession with the ease an on-the-job departmental transfer. Indeed, this is the indignity that the world's greatest Rollerball player, Jonathan E. (James Caan), has suffered...and never forgiven. He still loves his wife, but an executive in Italy had more power and stature...and took her. And she was paid handsomely to leave Jonathan, rewarded with a villa in Rome, and extreme wealth.

Early in "Rollerball," the company – represented by John Houseman's stern executive, Bartholomew – also delivers another despotic edict: Jonathan must retire from the game for "the common good." This demand doesn't sit well with Jonathan E., and he encourages his ever-increasing fame on the court, even in the face of attempts by the company to kill him.

Before long, Jonathan finds the corporation changing the game's rules on him. First, the Executive Class eliminates penalties for rough play. Then it eliminates replacements/substitutions, so that no injured players can leave the game in progress. Then, finally, the corporate men push a game with no established time limit. The final Rollerball game ends only when the last man is standing...

As you might expect, the Rollerball tournaments serve, in many ways, as the highlights of this classic sci-fi film. Staged with meticulous attention-to-detail and with an eye towards speed and acceleration, these games grow increasingly violent throughout the film. The set-piece against the Tokyo team, in particular, descends into a blood bath. One player even catches fire before the game is done.

If possible, the film's climactic contest – New York vs. Jonathan E.'s Houston team – is even more vicious. Scarlet blood is seen spilled all over the game arena, and in one horrible moment, the first aid responders are actually run down by a speeding motorcycle. Then our protagonist, Jonathan, kills a player right in front of Houseman's character, and before a live

TV audience.

All the while, a packed house cheers and applauds wildly over the violent action...

"Jonathan, there's one thing you ought to know, and nobody's said it, but I'm sure of it. They're afraid of you, Jonathan. All the way to the top, they are."

On one level, of course, "Rollerball" satirizes the hyperkinetic, overtly-commercialized world of modern organized sports, where the strongest, hunkiest lunkhead (Tim Tebow?) receives the most admiration based on the size of his... muscle mass.

This notion of making athletes "heroes" is made clear in a "Rollerball" scene set inside a locker room, as Bartholomew speaks to the players' egos. "They dream they're great Rollerballers," he tells them, speaking of Executives. "They dream they're Jonathan; they have muscles, they bash in faces."

On the other hand, and on a much deeper thematic level, "Rollerball" muses directly on the topic of freedom in a technological, mass-media Adams) makes a point relative to life in the 1970s and today. Ella asks Jonathan why he simply doesn't do what the Executives want him to do especially since he would be paid handsomely for his compliance.

Jonathan notes that it is a choice "between having nice things... or freedom." Ella responds – terrifyingly – "But comfort is freedom."

By contrast, Jonathan suggests the truth: "That's never been it. I mean, them privileges just buy us off."

In other words: Don't sweat things like individual freedom or liberty. There are items to purchase, things to own. Don't you want an Italian villa?

Incidentally, this very-"Rollerball" sentiment was mirrored rather dramatically in President Jimmy Carter's famous and much-derided "Crisis of Confidence" speech five years later, in 1979. He said:

"In a nation that was proud of hard work, strong families, close-knit communities, and our faith in God, too many of us now tend to worship self-indulgence and consumption. Human identity is no longer defined by what one does, but by what one owns. But we've discovered that owning things and consuming things does not satisfy our longing for meaning. We've learned that piling up material goods cannot fill the emptiness of lives which have no confidence or purpose."

"Rollerball" depicts a society in which the people have indeed accepted control by a ruling elite...in return for being "provided for," in return for "privilege."

But, in accordance with the President Carter quote, these same people have no sense of meaning or purpose.

Part of the reason the people live with such an unjust arrangement is because of a deliberate blackout of educational materials and information. Rollerball tournaments play endlessly on the television, and local libraries are impersonal computer centers that feature only "summaries" of important literary works and ideas.

Instead, the corporations own history itself: "What do you want books for?" Jonathan's team-mate, Moon Pie, asks innocently. "Look Johnny, if you wanna learn somethin', just get a Corporate Teacher to come and teach it to ya'. Use yer Privilege Card..."

It's clearly an Internet-less world, and in one scene in the film, Jonathan E. goes to Geneva to visit a computerized archive where all the answers about "corporate rule" are purported to exist. Not surprisingly, the computer librarian, named Zero, proves absolutely unhelpful in providing such data. In fact, the machine has lost the totality of the "13th Century" in terms of knowledge. Thus, there is no place to turn to in this world to learn about history, science, or nature. Everything is the game. Everything is blood lust.

Because as long as you think about the game, and which team is winning or losing, you aren't thinking about who is gaming the system and for what agenda.

Based on William Harrison's short story, "The Roller Ball Murder" (1973; Esquire), "Rollerball" runs for over two hours, and it features essentially two modes. The first mode reveals the kind of listless, purposeless, meaningless existence of "comfortable" citizens like Jonathan E. The second mode involves the game matches themselves, set on a circular track. The game play is urgent, pointed and murderous, a deliberate contrast to the film's lackadaisical first mode. I imagine that some audiences today would probably find these aspects of the film boring, but as the first mode concerns the existential angst of a futuristic gladiator, the insight into his daily life and routine is entirely appropriate.

Uniquely, "Rollerball" also makes widespread use of classical music, including Bach's "Toccata and Fugue in D minor," and "Adagio in G minor" from Tomaso Albinoni. These musical selections comment on the action (and understand the action) in a way that the film's knowledge-challenged dramatis personae cannot. The music – so distinctly of the human past – connects Jonathan E's futuristic struggle for freedom to such struggles in man's long history, and arises specifically from the Baroque tradition, dealing intentionally with the "affect of man." The musical selection that opens the film, Toccata and Fugue, renders the accompanying imagery (of game preparations in the vast Rollerball stadium) almost religious in stature and transmits the idea that we are witnessing an important ritual being played out.

"Rollerball"'s production design is, accordingly, relatively impersonal and dehumanizing in nature. Citizens visit vast "luxury centers," mall-like locations – places to shop – in keeping with such kindred fare as "Logan's Run" (1976). The Executive Suites as seen in the film are palatial and extravagant. The opulent lifestyle of the Executive Class is revealed in one dinner party scene, and the sequence ends with the drunken, entitled elite mindlessly blowing up trees with futuristic guns.

The Rollerball arena is itself an important metaphor in the film. The track is a loop, a track that never ends, with no end and no beginning. Teams battle one another for supremacy, going around and around on this track endlessly (kind of like a NASCAR race, I suppose). But one individual – a Spartacus of the future age – breaks out of this circular trajectory and takes the fight right to the stands.

One spectacularly effective composition in the Jewison film finds Jonathan E. braced against a transparent wall on the Rollerball rink. Behind him is Bartholomew, the executive, scowling. And reflected on the transparent glass are out-of-control flames

Here we have all three critical elements: the gladiator, the villain who is "untouchable" and the fire of revolt – of individual achievement – threatening to burn out of control.

The enduring genius of "Rollerball," I would submit, is that it artfully exposes how powerful people become addicted to controlling the lives of others The corporate stooges of the Executive Class wage full-bore, murderous war against a citizen because they want one player – one damned player – to retire from "their" game. They apparently don't consider tolerating Jonathan E's presence for a few more years, followed, presumably, by a peaceful retirement. Instead they seek to dominate and defeat Jonathan E. – a champion and competitor – and in doing so, incite his sense of competition.

For Jonathan, "Four or five little things make one big thing," and the retirement demand, on top of the loss of his wife to an executive, constitutes a tipping point. By pushing the stubborn and tough Jonathan E. to his line in the sand, the Corporate Culture only assures that Jonathan E. proves the very point they don't want established:

The will of the individual matters.

Cult-Movie Review: Quintet (1979)

(By John Kenneth Muir Copyright © John Kenneth Muir)

In the year 1979, director Robert Altman (1925-2006) teamed with star Paul Newman (1925-2008) to present one of the bleakest post-apocalyptic and dystopian cinematic visions ever forged, the wintry "Quintet."

Set well into a fictional future ice age of devastating "global cooling," "Quintet" was not received warmly by either film critics or audiences at the time of the film's theatrical release, and that perception has remained largely unchanged today. Indeed, "Quintet" is not an easy or particularly fun film to experience. The narrative moves at an almost glacial pace and the action features long periods of bracing, uncomfortable silence.

In addition to these qualities, Altman's feature boasts a kind of overt "icy" visual palette, with out-of-focus "cold" atmosphere encroaching visibly on the four corners of the frame. This unique, misty canvas is actually an ideal reflection of the film's existential crisis: that mankind is being suffocated spiritually and physically by the re-glaciation of all corners of the planet.

For some viewers, this misty, frost-bitten visual presentation will add immeasurably to the creeping sense of bleakness and claustrophobia Altman toils so assiduously to generate. For others, the effect may only serve to annoy or even distance one from the action on-screen.

Yet "Quintet" is a film worthy of patience, one crafted with real dedication, and with seemingly no consideration for commercial interests. The film is not merely bleak, it is intentionally, irrevocably hopeless. It goes out of its way, actually, to kill off "hope" in the first act. With cutthroat efficiency, "Quintet" depicts a world where the word "friend" has been replaced with the word "alliance," and then goes even further than that. In most post-apocalyptic movies, there is some opportunity for characters to escape, locate a sanctuary, or carve out at least some slice of small happiness. But without apology or explanation, "Quintet" asks audiences to countenance a future world in which there is no escape route, and each new day is just one cycle closer to inevitable extinction.

Another way to describe this artistic but difficult genre film: it's an intriguing place to visit, but you certainly would not want to live there.

"I Broke No Rules!"

As "Quintet" commences, a middle-aged seal hunter, Essex (Newman), and his young companion, the pregnant, innocent Vivia (Brigitte Fossey), make for a northern city, one of the last hubs of human civilization following a global cooling phenomenon that has turned all the Earth to inhospitable ice.

Essex seeks out his long-estranged brother, Francha (Thomas Hill), inside the ruined city, and learns that he is involved in a "Tournament," a game of Quintet, but with a few interesting and deadly additions.

In the traditional game of Quintet, five players attempt to move their pieces across a five-sided board and to finish off the other four players, following a "killing order" list. When four competitors are vanquished, the survivor then must fight "the sixth man," another player who has been waiting the duration of the game in "limbo," the space between the sides.

This extremely popular board game fits in with a new philosophical view, a quasi-religion that has gained adherents in this post-apocalyptic world without sustenance, without meaningful work, and without purpose. In particular, the five sides of the Quintet board represent the five stages of life: the pain of birth, the labor of maturing, the guilt of living, the terror of aging, and the finality of death.

But in the space between these five sides – in the limbo – there is a sixth stage of existence. It is an empty, black void that represents "total madness" and the awareness of a consuming nothingness. A preacher inside the city, St. Christopher (Vittorio Gassman), calls this sixth space the void that both precedes human life and the void that succeeds such life.

By understanding and accepting this void, he suggests, the people who dwell in this New Ice Age should "cherish the interruption;" cherish the icy misery they face each and every day. In other words, a slow death in an icy hell is infinitely preferable to the eternity of oblivion that bookends our existence. At least in the frozen new Ice Age, man can feel and think and breathe.

When an overly-competitive Quintet player named Redstone rolls a deadly explosive into Francha's home quarters and murders both Essex's brother and the delightful, youthful, Vivia, Essex realizes that the players in this Quintet tournament have forsaken the niceties of the board. This is now a game played with real lives, and in the real five sectors of this old, half-destroyed metropolis. Each of five players (plus a shadowy sixth man...) is attempting to kill each other and thus "win" the tournament.

Angry and confused, Essex joins the game, posing as Redstone. He checks into the Hotel Electra and soon meets the referee for the tournament, the flamboyant Grigor (Fernando Rey). Grigor wishes he could play in the tournament himself rather than merely "interpreting" the rules for the other players. He sees Essex – an impostor – as one fresh way to spice up the tournament, and therefore allows Essex to move freely about, encountering the other "players": the foolish Goldstar (David Langton), the ambitious Deuca (Nina Van Pallandt), and the seemingly helpful, if remote, Ambrosia (Bibi Andersson).

It is Ambrosia who warns Essex that the most dangerous opponent in the game is actually St. Christopher, a man who runs a religious mission espousing his world view and who believes whole-heartedly in the philosophy of Quintet.

As the players begin to die – murdered by one another – Essex seeks to understand the game even as his very existence is threatened. He is, perhaps, taken aback when he learns the identity of the invisible "sixth man" in this particular game...

I am not here to help or regard. I am here to interpret the rules.

The underlying idea for the film's post-apocalyptic world arises out of the scientific and media history of the 1970s.

In the early years of the disco decade, scientists began to become aware of a cooling trend on Earth, one that existed between the years 1945 and 1975, roughly. Popular news outlets jumped on the idea that a new ice age could be dawning, replete with a re-glaciation of the planet.

In summer of 1974, *TIME* magazine featured an article called "Another Ice Age," and worried about a "global climactic upheaval" as the "interglacial period" that had nurtured and nourished mankind for all his history came to an abrupt end. In 1975, *Newsweek* followed up with an equally alarming article called "The Cooling World." A hot seller at book-vendors in the same era was called *The Weather Conspiracy: The Coming of a New Ice Age*.

"Quintet" is set in a world where Mother Nature herself has literally turned a cold shoulder to mankind, and our cities, roads, railroads and grassy fields are buried under un-ending layers of frigid ice. Altman's film opens and closes with exterior views of white-on-white eternity as human figures wander into and out of view, respectively. The white-on-white opening and closing shots of the film mirror the existentialist, nihilistic philosophy of the Quintet board game: the film's action occurs in the "interlude" between the twin abysses, before-birth, and after-death.

Enhancing the sense of grim, unrelenting hopelessness, "Quintet" introduces us to the character of Vivia, a charming, child-like girl who approaches every new vista in the half-buried city with a sense of innocent wonder. Vivia is younger than any other survivor, perhaps the youngest of all the humans left alive on Earth, and she is pregnant. Her pregnancy – like her very personhood – carries our one hope for the future; that mankind can somehow carry on and survive in the face of an enveloping Ice Age. Even Vivia's name suggests life itself, derived from the Latin verb, vivere, meaning "to live."

When Vivia – life herself – is wantonly murdered in the movie's first act, all hope for a positive future is utterly destroyed. Essex may survive for a time, but it is not accurate to suggest that he really "lives." His life becomes devoted to Quintet; towards understanding the brand of death that took away his companion and his child; and the very future itself.

The murderer, Redstone, who killed both Vivia and her unborn child has no moral response to Essex's pursuit. After killing a roomful of innocents as well as his quarry (Francha), Redstone can only offer the worthless, pitiful caveat, "I broke no rules." If life and death are just part of a game, and murder is part of the rules, then perhaps he's right.

Virtually every character Altman introduces audiences to in "Quintet" clearly lives with the expectation that the world is coming to an end for the human race. "Hope is an obsolete word," one character notes truthfully. Even the film's final punctuation, Grigor's explanation about the "prize" if you win the Quintet Tournament, is woefully grim. Specifically, there is no cash reward, no cache of food, not even a warm jacket at the end of this game of death.

No, the winning "prize" to this death game is that you live to fight another day; you survive in a hopeless world for one more cycle, at least. That's the apotheosis of spirituality that these humans strive to achieve: one more day of misery, alive, before inevitably returning to the abyss of nothingness.

At the end of the film, Essex pointedly attempts to refute this kind of nihilist thinking, saying he prefers to hope for something better up north. But even this forced, vocal expression of hope is a sham. The next shot – the film's final, lingering image – finds Essex marching away into the white-on-white, snow-covered distance. He eventually disappears, gone in the haze, and the end credits roll. Essex may believe he has hope; but the abyss nonetheless swallows him in the end; as it swallows everyone.

In depicting a future world where there is as little humanity as there is warmth, "Quintet" ultimately proves distancing on an emotional level.

Paul Newman plays his character's emotions close-to-the-vest, going for a minimalist approach that denies us any significant level of understanding or sympathy. We want to watch him fall apart; to mourn with him over the death of the future. We want to watch him get even; watch him kill his enemies. But Newman's impressive, balanced performance permits no such easy solace; Essex carries his pain inside.

Even the murder and chase scenes in "Quintet" lack suspense (as critic Vincent Canby noted in *The New York Times*), but again, that seems to – oddly – fit the film's tenor. This world is so miserable and the character motivations so opaque, that we feel no thrill at either Essex's victory, or at St. Christopher's defeat. Our blood has run as cold as the landscape. The chill is so strong that while watching "Quintet" we begin to lose our capacity to feel for the characters, just as they have lost the capacity to empathize or sympathize with their fellow man.

The most human and affecting moment in **"Quintet"** occurs shortly after Vivia's death. By this point, Altman has staged multiple shots of dog packs *eating* human corpses, unbothered by the city goers. The dogs hungrily lick spilled blood out of the ice, and not a single human being attempts to stop the animals from feasting on such remains.

But the grieving Essex returns to his brother's quarters and takes the corpse of his companion Vivia (who was also carrying his child) and at great physical labor carries her body across the vast, open ice plain. The dog packs nip at his heels the whole way, but Essex finally reaches a freezing river, and disposes of Vivia's corpse there. *We watch as her body disappears beneath the placid surface*, and recognize this is an infinitely preferable end than the one society would otherwise have granted for her, as – *again literally* – dog food. And again, we don't see Essex break down or cry, or swear vengeance.

He just watches the body sink, and moves on.

It's tough – and yes, uncomfortable – to buy into a world where human life means so little that the bodies of loved ones are regularly left as food for scavengers, yet **"Quintet"** proves impressive on at least an intellectual level, perhaps because of its uncompromising nature. The bleak film plays in some ways like a bizarre Western, with a stranger arriving in a frontier town and becoming involved in a shoot-out contest, or some such thing, should such a comparison serve to contextualize the film for the wary.

So it's a challenge to "enjoy" **"Quintet,"** but as one character in the film trenchantly notes, *"You never understand the scheme until you are part of the scheme."* In other words, if you hunker down and truly commit to Altman's uncompromising vision for **"Quintet,"** you may come, in some cerebral fashion at least, to appreciate the terrifying and lonely world he shows you here.

Cult-Movie Review: Mad Max (1979)

(By John Kenneth Muir Copyright © John Kenneth Muir)

"They say people don't believe in heroes anymore…"

- Mad Max (1979)

Despite multitudinous descriptions to the contrary, George Miller and Byron Kennedy's "Mad Max" (1979) is not actually a post-apocalyptic film.

Rather, it's pre-apocalyptic. But the handwriting is certainly on the wall…and on the open roads.

This celebrated cult film might more accurately be described as dystopian in conception because the filmmakers imagine a world, "a few years from now," in which widespread lawlessness has taken hold, and the authorities – increasingly more fascist in tone, powers, and demeanor – are helpless to prevent a culture-wide death spiral into anarchy and chaos.

Dominated by a caustic aesthetic of anticipatory anxiety, a sense of psychic uneasiness that suffuses every frame, "Mad Max" is literally a movie about mankind speeding – foot pressed hard against the pedal – towards moral and spiritual annihilation.

Often, I compare Miller's "Mad Max" to the early cinematic endeavors of Wes Craven ("Last House on the Left") and Tobe Hooper ("The Texas Chainsaw Massacre") because there's a genuine feeling while watching "Mad Max" that you, yourself, are in peril. As is the case with Craven or Hooper, the audience feels jeopardized in Miller's hands, as though it might end up seeing something that could truly do the psyche harm.

At one point in the film, our hero – police officer and family man Max (Mel Gibson) – admits that he's "scared," and the audience wholly shares that trepidation. Max's vicious world is one without a safety net, in which the laws of the jungle dominate. Miller enthusiastically takes the film beyond the bounds of movie decorum and good taste right from the start – from the opening sequence – and leaves viewers wondering just how far he will tread into taboo territory.

The result is a film that has lost none of its dreadful, visceral power in over three decades.

"Look, any longer out on that road and I'm one of them, a terminal psychotic, except that I've got this bronze badge that says that I'm one of the good guys. "

"Mad Max" opens, both symbolically and literally, on Anarchie (Anarchy) Road, as leather-clad members of the under-staffed MFP (Main Force Patrol) pursue a dangerous "terminal psychotic" called Nightrider.

Nightrider believes himself a "fuel-injected suicide machine," and survives all attempts at pursuit and restraint. At least that is, until Max (Gibson) – the best – joins the chase.

Finally, Nightrider is killed in a high-speed wreck. Unfortunately, his "friends," led by the gang leader, Toecutter, desire vengeance. One of Toecutter's minions, Johnny, is apprehended by Max's friend, Officer Goose (Steve Bisley), but then released by effete, officious lawyers. Next, it is Goose who becomes a target for Toecutter's mad revenge.

After Goose is burned and maimed on the road by Toecutter, Max resigns from the force. With his wife Jesse (Joanne Samuel) and young son in tow, he heads out on a vacation from his responsibilities. Unfortunately, Max's family almost immediately crosses paths with Johnny, Toecutter and the others, and pays the ultimate price. Max's wife and son are run down on the open road, and left dying.

Enraged, and with no legal recourse, Max takes command of a souped-up police interceptor, and engages his enemies on the open highway, outside the bounds and restrictions of the law.

I'm not a bad man. I'm sick. I've got a personality disorder...

As is the case with all works of art, this film arises from a very specific context.

In particular, "Mad Max" emerges from the era of "Oz-ploitation" or the so-called Australian New Wave, which included such works as Peter Weir's "Picnic at Hanging Rock." But more specifically, "Mad Max" is very deliberately a reflection of the events, trends and fads of the early 1970s.

As co-writer James McCausland has acknowledged, much of the film's anarchic energy is fueled by the 1973 Oil Crisis, in which OPEC reduced oil production and quickly sent world economies into a tailspin. As gas supplies were rationed, McCausland apparently saw reports of violent outbreaks at gas stations, where drivers acted decisively (and aggressively...) to assure that they weren't caught short at the pump.

Also critical to the formation of "Mad Max's" underlying structure, no doubt, was "The Super-Car Scare" of 1972 - 1973, which occurred at the height of muscle car culture in Australia. There were talks at that time, indeed, of new vehicles that could travel 160 miles an hour, as well as news story accounts of young, out-of-control drivers in muscle cars (small cars with big, powerful engines...) racing through small communities and causing civil and traffic disturbances.

If you also acknowledge a bit of punk influence here – courtesy of the nihilistic music movement on blazing ascent, circa 1974 -1976 – you can easily detect how all the creative ingredients for "Mad Max" fall into place. Suddenly, we have punk criminals prowling the highways of Australia in souped-up super vehicles, vying for both the remaining oil supply and day-by-day, moment-to-moment domination. One scene in the film explicitly joins all contexts: Toecutter and his gang hijack a gas trunk on the road, and siphon precious gas from the storage tank. The underlying message is of a corrupt but rising youth movement leeching off and destroying a dying establishment.

If "No Future" was the unofficial credo and soundtrack of punk music in those days of the disco decade, "Mad Max" remains the most potent visualization of living for the moment, on impulse, and entirely for self. This is what the law of the jungle is, as dramatized by Toecutter and his gang. He is a man with no respect for life, law, family, or community. All he cares about is getting what he wants when he wants it. "Anything I say? What a wonderful philosophy you have," he quips to a cowering victim.

The world has gone to Hell in a hand basket in "Mad Max," and those who still play by the old rules of law try to understand what has happened, and struggle to play catch-up "Here I am, trying to put sense to it, when I know there isn't any," Max notes, importantly, after the death of Goose. He's dealing here with a world that no longer makes sense to him.

Accordingly, Max progressively loses his faith that society's decaying infrastructure (as represented by the ramshackle local police center or "halls of justice") can stop the world from spiraling towards destruction.

It's clear Max's loss of faith arises for a reason, and is not some personal, solitary angst. His boss, Fifi (Roger Ward), keeps mentioning the need for heroes, and the culture's absence of heroes.

But what heroes, honestly, could possibly inhabit a blighted, decrepit police station like his?

The nihilism of the world, of "the terminal psychotics" seems to have bled the life out of public institutions in "Mad Max," leaving them as rotting monuments to a previous golden age. Max realizes, appropriately, that Fifi's comments are "crap." What his world needs is not cowboy heroes, but a functioning infrastructure; one that funds the police, trains the police, and supports the police in the battle against crime.

Although the lawyers and judicial officers glimpsed in "Mad Max" are portrayed as effete, intellectual egg-heads with their heads-up-their-asses, the police are not viewed in terms much more friendly. In the film's first scene, we catch a young MFP officer ogling a couple making love, and then indulging in a high speed chase which endangers other officers, and civilians. He looks like he could be a gang member himself...except he's wearing a leather cop uniform. Similarly, Fifi is interested only in results, not the letter of the law. He just wants the paperwork to be "clean" so he doesn't get in trouble with superiors. Again, the impression is of an old, once noble institution that has given way to corruption and decrepitude.

Again and again in the film, Max sees evil triumph over the (flawed) forces of order, and so must make a fateful decision about his own place and role in the world. "Mad Max" thus brilliantly diagrams one man's disillusionment about society, and his final, knowing, unfortunate break from it. Many see the film as being fascist in viewpoint because the criminals attempt to argue that they are merely "sick" (and thus to be treated with compassion), but I disagree with that assessment. Max gets revenge, but at what price?

The price is the very eventuality that Max so dramatically fears all along. He knows, even starting out, that there is very little difference between the cops and the "terminal psychotics" who vie for control of the roadways. When Max's family and friends die, that line is blurred entirely. Max realizes, contra Fifi, that there can no longer be any heroes. Heroes only work in context of a functioning civilization and support system.

As critic Keith Phipps astutely intimated, "Mad Max" is almost a character piece, a tale of a man trying to figure out where he belongs under the rules of the New World (Dis)Order:

"Only Mel Gibson, given the best entrance since Clint Eastwood in A Fistful of Dollars, has the ability to stand in the way, and from the start Miller links that ability to an appetite for self-destruction. It takes a while for that appetite to manifest itself fully, however. Miller places his hero at the center of a three-way tug of war between the violent anarchy of the outlaw, the barely suppressed fascism of the authorities, and the domestic comforts of his wife and child."

I often write here about how deeply and thoroughly I disapprove of movies that utilize revenge as the primary motivation for heroes or superheroes. I think that's just pandering to an ugly, ignoble impulse in human beings. In this case, however, I would argue that "Mad Max" does not glamorize revenge and, on the contrary, sends its wayward hero off into a form of societal banishment for his transgression. Max ends up in the wilderness/wasteland, seeking redemption for his voluntary break from the mores of a (admittedly crumbling) society (see: "The Road Warrior"). It takes him two more films, essentially, to reconnect with his more noble human nature.

So yes, Max gets his bloody vengeance in this film, but his ultimate fear is realized too. In breaking the laws of civilization, the only difference between him and the Toecutter's minions remains that he possesses a bronze badge. What would his wife and son think of him now?

The final shot of "Mad Max" consists, not coincidentally, of an open and empty road. We race down it going ever faster, but never actually arriving at a destination. There is no love and no companionship on this long road. Max now lives for no one but himself. He can look forward to isolation, mistrust, and confrontation...but nothing else; at least nothing good or positive.

This is a threshold moment...

While carefully noting what he believed was "Mad Max's" sense of amorality, *Chicago Reader* film critic Dave Kehr also accurately described the film as some "of the most determinedly formalist filmmaking this side of Michael Snow."

What that description means, in lay terms, is that Mad Max isn't about dispassionately recording or realistically chronicling the details of its sparse, almost Western-styled narrative. Rather, it's about making the audience feel strong emotions. Namely fear, rage and even, briefly, bloodlust.

The reasons behind "Mad Max's" passionate, singular approach to filmmaking are actually, I believe, entirely moral.

As the film's villain, Toecutter (Hugh Keays-Byrne) notes to an underling named Johnny (Tim Burns), an act of brutal murder can be considered a "threshold moment" in terms of the human soul. That's his philosophy of life. There's no future. There's no common good. There's just the shattering of boundaries, until everything – and everyone – is wrecked.

Now, a threshold is widely defined as the point at which a physiological or psychological effect begins to be produced, and that seems to be precisely what Toecutter is fostering in both his friends and his enemies. He is sponsoring and encouraging madness, psychosis and violence. Indeed, there seems to be a plague of madness and nihilism sweeping the world in this film, and Toecutter fosters it in his cohorts (such as Nightrider) and his protégé (Johnny).

In the film's climax, the audience's surrogate – Max himself – endures a similar "threshold moment," treading literally and metaphorically into morally "prohibited" territory (as a street sign indicates) just as he is about to cross-the-line of legality. The fearsome legend on the sign literally warns him to stop (lest he become like Toecutter), but Max ignores it.

This particular bit of clever framing (pictured above) is not an accident. Max crosses a moral and geographical boundary in search of personal satisfaction, and Miller's shot deliberately evokes an earlier one in the film, set on a lovely beach.

There, Toecutter and his gang have similarly ignored signs and warnings about transgression, and headed off knowingly into forbidden territory. The point of the nearly identical staging seems to be that Max – in taking the law into his own hands – is following the very nihilistic path he fears.

"Mad Max" is actually a moral film, I submit, because it concerns that threshold moment in each of us, too. Vengeance might be sated. But after the vengeance? As "Last House on the Left" observed, post-violence, "the road leads to nowhere, and the castle stays the same." In other words, there's a very big difference between portraying violence and approving of violence. I would argue "Mad Max" (brilliantly) portrays violence, while never, even for a moment, glamorizing it or approving of it.

Instead, "Mad Max" asks: what comes with moral transgression? How does a crossing of the "threshold moment" affect a good person? And if good people can willingly cross the threshold to barbarism, what becomes of civilization, a social concept erected on the foundation of the common good, not personal retribution?

"Mad Max" gazes at all these ideas, but does so while moving at 150 miles-an-hour.

The film – heightened immeasurably by Brian May's superb score and George Miller's orchestration of the high-speed stunts – conveys a powerful sense not just of speed, but of speeding out of control. "Mad Max" also reveals a world falling apart at the seams, but doesn't offer pat explanations for the breakdown, or easy answers about the solution. We can try to "put sense" to the madness of this world, but there is quite definitively no sense behind the human impulse towards self-destruction.

If "Mad Max" is right, the world itself is terminally psychotic.

Cult-Movie Review: The Terminator (1984)

(By John Kenneth Muir Copyright © John Kenneth Muir)

"This is burned in by laser scan. Some of us were kept alive... to work... loading bodies. The disposal units ran night and day. We were that close to going out forever. But there was one man who taught us to fight, to storm the wire of the camps, to smash those metal motherfuckers into junk. He turned it around. He brought us back from the brink. His name is Connor. John Connor. Your son, Sarah, your unborn son."

- Kyle Reese (Michael Biehn) in The Terminator (1984)

Today we travel back in time – to the distant year 1984 – and to Jim Cameron's first smash-hit motion-picture, the science-fiction action thriller: "The Terminator." This intense, fast-moving film not only began Cameron's career in Hollywood, it vaulted star Arnold Schwarzenegger to super-stardom (following the "Conan" films) and even gave him a recurring catchphrase: "I'll be back."

Speaking to the film's quality and longevity, "The Terminator" has spawned five movie sequels (in 1991, 2003, 2009, 2015, and 2019 respectively) and even a spin-off TV series: "The Sarah Connor Chronicles." Also, the Library of Congress added "The Terminator" in 2008 to its National Film Registry, marking the film as culturally, aesthetically, and historically significant.

An ugly incident in the film's history involves a threatened lawsuit from late science fiction legend Harlan Ellison, who claimed that "The Terminator" ripped-off elements of Ellison's The Outer Limits episode "Soldier," the second season premiere that featured two future soldiers accidentally traveling to the present and battling one another. The matter was settled out of court, and Ellison's name was added to the film's end credits, apparently over Cameron's urging to Orion to fight the matter.

This matter acknowledged, there's no way to gaze at "The Terminator" as anything other than the product of James Cameron's stellar visual and storytelling imagination. Looking back across the decades, it's plain to see how his film fits in with the remainder of his oeuvre, and introduces his career-long obsessions with strong women, star-crossed lovers, fish-out-of-water protagonists, and the bugaboo of nuclear war.

Going back to the original "Terminator" in 2019 it's a little amazing just how well the film holds up. In many senses, it holds up even better than does its 1991 follow-up, "Judgment Day." The action scenes here are still breathtaking, the love story remains affecting, and the film features a relentless, driving sense of urgency. Indeed, "The Terminator" never lets up, never stops, never looks back...much like its titular character.

And yet, gazing beneath the surface, one can detect the unconventional but canny manner in which Cameron approaches the film, and how his directorial strategy buttresses the quality of the piece substantially. For instance, there are relatively few conventional locales or settings featured in the film at all. This is a movie that takes place in parking garages, in speeding vehicles, inside seedy motels, in sewers, and in smoke-filled police station waiting areas. The film never truly settles down in any one place too long, and that fact actually contributes to the driving pulse of the piece. You feel like the movie has been made on the fly, filmed in one brief sanctuary after another, as the protagonists' safety is constantly eclipsed and imperiled.

Secondly, "The Terminator" creates – at times – this weird, almost authentically dream-like vibe. It arises from the conjunction of Brad Fiedel's effective synthetic score, and Cameron's frequent use of slow-motion photography to extend time and mine the latent tension in many sequences. Time, of course, is the very crux of the film, and the way that Cameron stretches and bends time matters a great deal in the film's overall artistic tapestry.

Heroes Kyle Reese and Sarah Connor only share just "one night" together, as the film's dialogue reminds the audience, and yet they experience a "lifetime" of love. This is not merely romantic hyperbole. It's an accurate expression of how deeply the audience comes to sympathize with the heroes and their doomed relationship. James Cameron's choice of techniques reminds us that it's not how much time we have that matters, but what we make with the time we're given. His directorial flourish – slow-motion photography, particularly – is a perfect example of form highlighting or reflecting content.

A near-perfect fusion of big emotions, big concepts and stellar action-movie filmmaking, it's almost impossible to conceive of "The Terminator" as Cameron's first, since it remains so accomplished on so many fronts.

Come with me if you want to live.

In the year 2029 A.D., the human survivors of a devastating nuclear war are on the verge of defeating their enemy, an artificial intelligence called SkyNet.

In response, the intelligent machine sends a cyborg called a Terminator (Arnold Schwarzenegger) back in time to the year 1984 to kill waitress Sarah Connor (Linda Hamilton), who will one day be the mother of the future resistance leader, General John Connor.

The resistance responds to this initiative by sending back to 1984 someone to stop the killing machine, a foot soldier named Kyle Reese (Michael Biehn).

In 1984, the Terminator uses the phone book and begins to methodically kill all L.A. residents named Sarah Connor. As the police (Paul Winfield and Lance Henriksen) assemble the disturbing clues in the case and grow concerned they're dealing with a serial killer, an unwitting Sarah encounters the Terminator at a club called Tech Noir.

Kyle rescues Sarah and soon tells her the story of the future not yet written; of her unborn son, John, and her tutelage of him in the ways of war.

But even as Kyle and Sarah fall in love, the Terminator continues his relentless drive to find them and murder Sarah. After decimating an entire police station, the Terminator pursues an injured Kyle and Sarah on the road.

The final battle to decide the future occurs in an automated factory, Cyberdyne Systems...

Look at it this way: in a hundred years, who's gonna care?

Perhaps the very best quality about "The Terminator" is that it eerily and effectively crafts two very distinctive and atmospheric worlds.

The first such world is Los Angeles of 1984, and city life is dramatized here as this weird twilight-and-neon world of seemingly never-ending night.

The city boulevards are rain-soaked and wind-swept. Garbage blows continually through alleyways. Strangers, hobos and other fringe dwellers seem to move back and forth, half-conscious, in the neon-lit streets, unnoticed and un-commented upon. Here, in total anonymity, a monster arrives; a technological boogeyman that can change the direction of the future itself. But because he is human in appearance, he is perfectly disguised, able to fit in easily with the human flotsam and jetsam.

As Cameron paints it, this world feels particularly fragile and unwelcoming. '

The punk rock music (as heard in the club Tech Noir) is harsh and driving, and there's a feeling that the denizens of daytime such as Sarah Connor don't easily see or understand the denizens of the city's night. This is important, of course, because a war is being waged secretly at night. Two warriors - the Terminator and Kyle Reese – slip into this world and, unnoticed, fight for the very future of mankind. They pick off resources (clothing, weapons, groceries, etc.), and march forward on competing agendas. The overall feeling is that no one in authority is watching. Nobody cares. These people and their urban world have been written off as unimportant, inconsequential. This world, at least from the perspective of the future, is already dead, a metaphorical if not literal graveyard.

Cameron artfully picks up on a true 1980s aesthetic here, showcasing the homeless, the hopeless, and the lost as part of his twilight world. Other films in the 1980s such as "Vamp" (1986) and John Carpenter's "Prince of Darkness" (1987) and "They Live" (1988) capture a similar mood; the electric notion that another world co-exists with ours, and could intersect with our experience at any time. It's half-seen and half-acknowledged, but it's there…

The second world that "The Terminator" creates with frightening acumen is Los Angeles of 2029. It's a world in which human skulls appear to form the firmament of a new terrain, and the skies are forever gray and dark.

Many science fiction films visit post-apocalyptic futures, but "The Terminator" presents one of the grimmest and most effective visualizations of such a landscape. The world of 2029 is a colossal junkyard that consists of ruins as far as the eye can see. Where some films (such as "The Road Warrior" or the "Planet of the Apes" films) have opted for showcasing real deserts as the aftermath of a nuclear war, "The Terminator" really goes for broke here, showcasing broken, desperate humans living in horrible, miserable conditions. Man's world has been twisted and broken. In fact, it isn't man's world at all anymore.

One terrific shot in the post-apocalyptic scenes reveals two starving children huddling in front of a TV set. Cameron switches views after a minute, and we see the yellow light emanating from the television is that of a candle, one set inside the broken screen. The moment is picture perfect as gallows humor, and as heartbreaking glimpse of a tomorrow that must never be.

The feeling evoked in the contrast between 1984 and 2029 is that one world leads to the other world, as easily as the present flows into the future. There's a feeling in the 1980s scenes that mankind has abdicated his sense of responsibility to the world and to civilization at large. The police detectives, expertly-played by Paul Winfield and Lance Henriksen, are well-meaning but overworked and under-equipped. In one scene involving the police detectives, the question is asked "who is in charge here?" The answer seems to be nobody. Nobody is in charge. Nobody is making a difference. Man seems to have given up on his world and his fellow man. Again, there's the feeling that this world is already dead; its epitaph already written.

Sarah's roommate, Ginger, for instance, tunes out of reality even while making love to her boyfriend, Matt. And Sarah and others seem to constantly be speaking to answering machines or unfeeling telephone operators.

Punk-styled predators – played by Bill Paxton and Brian Thompson – stalk the night too, seizing on the world's very lack of order. It's not difficult, given the shape of the world of 1984, to imagine a future in which man surrenders his very well-being to a machine. Indeed, Tech Noir – the Night of Technology - precedes the dawn of SkyNet both metaphorically and literally in the film's chronology.

As I wrote in *Horror Films of the 1980s* (2007), "the antidote to this techno-punk world is human love and connection." And here, Cameron gives the audience star-crossed lovers Kyle and Sarah, two classic characters in film history.

They not only love each other, they conceive a savior for human-kind out of that love. Implicit in this scenario is a criticism of the world as it stands in the 1980s. It's one where, to quote Charlton Heston in "Planet of the Apes," there seems to be an abundance of lovemaking, but little real love.

Murder is as easy as flipping through a phone book (let your fingers do the walking...), the police are ineffective, and even medical science (as represented by Earl Boen's Dr. Silberman) is incapable of feeling empathy or providing help.

The seed Kyle brings back to Sarah, then, is one of love, compassion and self-sacrifice. Kyle is a man of duty who understands how valuable human life is, and he brings that understanding to a purposeless Sarah and to her disaffected, empty world.

Consider Kyle for a moment. He could have escaped from his apocalyptic world back to 1984 and made a very selfish decision. He could have stolen some clothes, abandoned his mission, and had a pretty decent life (at least until 1997). But Kyle didn't do that. He cared about his peers and his purpose and stuck to his mission of saving a woman he had never met, and only fantasized about.

In "Terminator 2," Sarah tells Silberman that everyone blindly living life (before Judgment Day) is already dead; and that's also clearly the vibe of "The Terminator." The world seems to be running on fumes, as a culture of death spirals further and further away from not just inter-connection, but civility and decency itself.

Reese opens Sarah's eyes to the fact that "a storm is coming," and that the world in this half-awake, half-asleep state, cannot continue. Sarah also opens up Kyle's eyes to love, too. She makes him see that he can't remain disconnected from pain or hurt, or that he'll be making the same mistake as the 1984-ers.

At several crucial junctures in "The Terminator," Cameron utilizes slow-motion photography to enhance the power of his visuals. In the first such case, the Terminator kicks open the door of a middle-aged woman named Sarah Connor (not our final girl, but another S.C....). He forces his way into the house, levels a gun at her head, and fires. It's all vetted in agonizing slow-motion, and so the nature of the intrusion and violation is heightened significantly. The terror of the moment – the seeming randomness of the crime – is punctuated. As the moment lingers, we reflect on the horror of it. Of a stranger coming to our door, breaking it down, and leveling a gun at us. Again, this is a very 1980s brand of fear: of random violence and crime run amok.

Later, Cameron uses slow-motion photography during the lead-up to the Tech Noir fight sequence, and this time he deploys it to lengthen the audience's feelings of tension and suspense. Sarah Connor has no one to protect her, no avenue of escape at all, and as the Terminator nears in slow-motion, his power and dominance – and her vulnerability – attain near-epic proportions.

Finally, Cameron uses slow motion photography at the culmination of Sarah and Kyle's love scene. Intertwined, their hands open slowly, as if a flower blooming. The idea here – again – is that time may be constant, but as humans we experience it as relative. Here, the connection between Sarah and Kyle is significant and meaningful, and the "blossoming" image of their hands suggests that their love has, well, literally borne fruit. Their love-making is also like a stolen moment during an un-ending nightmare that "will never be over."

In "The Terminator," one of Cameron's neatest conceits involves this manipulation of time's passage in the edit. And yes, it's a highly appropriate selection given the film's theme about time travel. Cameron's approach reminds us that time feels different at different times, and that ultimately the secret of time is to make something positive out of what time we have.

Over and over again in the film, Cameron reveals great ingenuity in how he deals with the concept of the future.

For example, Sarah's waitress friend notes that in a hundred years, no one will care about what's she doing in 1984, but that is not technically true. The people of 2029 no doubt wish that the denizens of that earlier age had made different choices, especially regarding the invention and implementation of SkyNet.

And personally, of course, Sarah Connor's name will no doubt be long known – even in 2084 – if human beings manage to defeat the smart machines.

Also, the film is downright poetic in the way it deals with Sarah Connor's photograph, and Kyle's possession/loss of it. Interestingly, we see the photo burn in the film before we even see it developed.

But we are asked by Reese to wonder what Sarah is thinking about when the picture is snapped. By the last reel, we know precisely: she's thinking of him, of Kyle. Thus Kyle fell in love with a photograph of a woman who, before he was ever born, was already in love with him. Mind-boggling stuff.

Other aspects of the film are equally stirring and admirable. For instance, the disintegration of the Terminator's human appearance is splendidly vetted. His eyebrows are singed off first. Then he loses an eye. Next he injures his forearm (and must repair it with a razor knife...). As the movie progresses, the Terminator appears less and less human, until finally – during the climax – he is revealed as the soulless automaton that he is, no longer able to pass in human society as one of us. The methodical disintegration of the Terminator's appearance, however, barely seems to go noticed by society at large, and again a point is made about people only seeing what they want to see; of avoiding the confrontation with something different or unpalatable.

Sarah Connor is also James Cameron's first great female character. She starts out living a largely un-examined life, and yet by the end of the film can clearly "see" a future that others can't. She survives the attack on her life and becomes the person she was destined to be. Although Sarah protests along the way of her development – noting that she can't even balance her checkbook – she soon becomes literally the mother of humanity's future.

The shadow of nuclear Armageddon hovers over "The Terminator," and that too is a common aspect of Cameron's canon. Nuclear weapons play a critical role in every one of his films save – for obvious reasons – "Titanic" (1997). Here, Cameron focuses on the madness of putting life-and-death nuclear decisions in the hands of "the machine," and that theme would become even more pronounced in the sequel.

But again, the context of this film must be named, and no offense is intended, just a recitation of facts. In the early eighties President Reagan sometimes joked about nuclear war. On an open mike he once declared that "bombing begins in five minutes," and in a 1984 debate with candidate Walter Mondale he inaccurately reported that nuclear missiles could be recalled from submarines after their launch. Many of his advisers in his first term stressed the concept of "winnable" nuclear war, and that's simply a terrifying thought. To President Reagan's ever-lasting credit, he backed down from these beliefs (and even recanted his "Evil Empire" comment) in the name of peace. Regardless of his welcome evolution, the "apocalypse mentality" of the 1980s was a hugely powerful force in American cinema mid-decade – think "War Games" (1983) and "Dreams-cape" (1984) – and one can see it here, very prominently, in "The Terminator."

I've also often likened "The Terminator" to a technological version of John Carpenter's "Halloween" (1978) because both films involve an unstoppable, relentless monster pursuing a young woman, and that woman's ultimate turnaround to fight back. Michael Myers is "The Shape" and not quite human, and Arnie's Terminator is a technological monster. But these boogeymen certainly share traits in common. They both come and go as they please; they both often hide in plain sight; and their thought processes are quite opaque to audiences. They both kill and pursue victims, but we don't really know what they're thinking or why they're thinking it. Like Michael, the Terminator – who also survives being beaten, bruised and flame-broiled – is truly a classic movie villain because of his relentless nature.

In the sequels, Arnold would play the machine as a hero, but there's something potent, callous and devious about his portrayal of this Terminator, this first time out. Underlying the cold, mechanical nature of the thing, there's some sense of an identity, of an enjoyment of his vile actions. This Terminator thrives on the hunt, it seems, and isn't entirely immune to concepts such as irony or humor. His selection of rejoinder to a nosy landlord in a sleazy motel is a perfect example. "Fuck you, asshole." Why select that particular option (from a table of options)? It has something to do, I would argue, with the machine's personality.

"The Terminator" is an incredibly effective thrill machine, but the reason the film is remembered today (and will be remembered well into the future) is because James Cameron has surrounded his meticulous action scenes with "living human tissue," namely an affecting love story and meditation on time itself. This skin on the story's mechanical bones makes the film resonate on a deeper level, and point explicitly towards Cameron's future approach in film making.

It's "something about the field generated by a living organism"... and it's called heart.

35 Years Ago: The Running Man (1987)

(By John Kenneth Muir Copyright © John Kenneth Muir)

"This is television, that's all it is. It has nothing to do with people, it's to do with ratings! For fifty years, we've told them what to eat, what to drink, what to wear. For Christ's sake, Ben, don't you understand? Americans love television. They wean their kids on it. Listen. They love game shows, they love wrestling, they love sports and violence. So what do we do? We give 'em what they want! We're number one, Ben, that's all that counts, believe me."

-Damon Killian, in The Running Man (1987)

Based on a 1982 sci-fi novel by Richard Bachman (Stephen King, actually), the motion picture version of "The Running Man" (1987) arrived in theaters during the Great Year of Arnold Schwarzenegger; the very season that also brought audiences John McTiernan's spectacular "Predator."

Although viewers typically and rightly associate Schwarzenegger with action and s.f. films, "The Running Man" ably – and rather surprisingly – functions best as a pointed satire of American television and politics.

While the writing and performances in this dystopian film tend towards the razor sharp, the action sequences in the film don't always hold up as well in terms of 21st century expectations. They feel episodic and repetitive. To be certain, the film is a highly entertaining experience from start to finish, but never, precisely, the adrenalin-inducing thrill ride that some action fans might hope for or expect.

Still, it seems the film's trademark action scenes did inspire a real life competition TV series titled "American Gladiators" (1989 -

1996), right down to the spandex costumes. Also, one might argue that the episodic nature of the action sequences in the film in some way mirrors the episodic nature of television programming, which adheres strictly to formula, as unalterable as death or taxes.

Bachman/King's literary version of "The Running Man" remains far more grim, serious and spectacular in approach than the Schwarzenegger film, a fact which makes the possibility of a more source-faithful movie adaptation a possibility, especially in this age of remakes. The novel is set in a totalitarian America in 2025 and involves a man, Ben Richards, "running" on a popular TV program so as to pay for expensive medicine for his ailing daughter.

The movie version eliminates this important character background and motivation, as well as the novel's incendiary, unforgettable ending; one which transforms Richards from a game show contestant to a bonafide enemy of the state, martyr and so-called "terrorist."

The 1987 movie version is less interested in creating real, identifiable characters and building a believable dystopian future world than it is in commenting humorously (if accurately) on aspects of our own culture. Not there's anything wrong with that.

Like I wrote above, it's the biting satire of American media and politics that makes "The Running Man" such a rewarding film to watch over twenty-five years after it was released. If anything, the film's observations about our entertainment seems only more apt in 2015, after we've all endured more than a decade of reality television programming.

The movie version of "The Running Man" actually has much more in common with Roger Corman and Paul Bartel's trail-blazing "Death Race 2000" (1975) than it does with King's literary portrait of a totalitarian future America.

In both "Death Race 2000" and "The Running Man," the media and the government have joined forces – through a popular TV show – to divert the attention of the poverty-stricken masses. While the country fails, these "bread and circuses" successfully keep the populace distracted from real problems, namely the class warfare between the haves and the have-nots. In both films, the popular TV show also overtly focuses on bloodshed and violence, either in the form of a cross-country race or a pedestrian chase.

Directed by Paul Michael Glaser, "The Running Man" also shares much in common with another great 1987 science fiction movie: Verhoeven's "RoboCop" (which I'll be reviewing next Tuesday).

Both cinematic endeavors feature short, satirical commercials and imagery that reveal, at length, how crass and stupid network television can really be. Ironically, considering Schwarzenegger's presence, "The Running Man" also shares "RoboCop's" anti-establishment suspicion of the ascendant right wing in America during the eighties.

Where "RoboCop" humorously depicted the end result of privatizing anything and everything in America, including the police force, "The Running Man" gazes more directly at the cult of celebrity in America and the ever-increasing blending of politics and entertainment.

Lest we forget it, a Hollywood actor was President of the United States in 1987 and, because of his advanced age, some folks considered him more a showman by many than an actual leader in terms of policy and administration. "The Running Man" takes that premise further, envisioning a wholesale blending of entertainment and politics at every level of government.

For instance, at one point in the film, Killian (game show host Richard Dawson) barks "Get me the Justice Department...Entertainment Division." In the same scene, he orders an underling to "get me the President's agent." In another sequence, "court-appointed talent agents" are discussed.

The idea here is that Hollywood and politics are a match made in Heaven (or is it Hell?). Both Hollywood and Washington D.C. focus on the same important task: selling imagery and fantasy, not reality, to an American populace desperately seeking hope, truth and justice.

The film is even more cynical than that description suggests. "The Running Man" posits that concepts such as justice are all just a game, anyway...a spin of the wheel of fortune.

And in the world of "The Running Man," freedom isn't even on the board. You can win such great prizes (if you're lucky...) as "trial by jury," "suspended sentence" and even "a full pardon," but real liberty is absent.

"I'm not into politics. I'm into survival."

"The Running Man" is set in the year 2019. The World Economy has collapsed and food, oil and natural resources are in short supply all over the United States.

Because of these crises, a police state has arisen in America. No dissent is tolerated, and television is controlled and created entirely by the State.

Helicopter pilot Ben Richards (Schwarzenegger) is arrested by his fellow officers when he refuses to open fire on unarmed civilians during an urban food riot. But the State manipulates video footage of this event and thus transforms the innocent Richards into "The Butcher of Bakersfield."

This is another example of government's manipulation of media, and media imagery in the film; the transformation of a real-life hero into a hissable villain for wide-scale public consumption. An easily digestible image or sound-bite is packaged and sold, rather than a possibly-damaging, harder-to-countenance reality.

Richards is sent to a work camp and spends the next eighteen months there. After an escape from the labor camp, Ben Richards is apprehended by authorities thanks to lovely Amber (Maria Conchita Alonso), a citizen who believes the lies about "The Butcher."

When Damon Killian (Dawson), host of the number one TV show, "The Running Man," sees news footage of Richards in action, the ratings-hungry showman realizes he's discovered the next great star. He quickly negotiates to have Ben Richards turned over to him.

Richards reluctantly appears on "The Running Man," a game show in which contestants run for their lives...against terrible odds. There, he is pitted against government "heroes" – really blood-thirsty killers –with names such as Sub-Zero, Bloodlust, Buzzsaw, Dynamite and Captain Freedom (Jesse Ventura).

However, if Richards can hook up with the People's Network, a growing resistance movement, and gain control of the "Running Man" transmission, Killian may have a few surprises coming his way...

"Mr. Richards, I'm your court-appointed theatrical agent."

"The Running Man" works overtime, and with more than a modicum of cleverness, to create a world in which image and reality don't match up.

Again, this is what I have often termed the Be Afraid, Be Very Afraid/Don't Worry Be Happy duality of the decade.

Americans were asked in the eighties to believe that they could spend (much) more on national defense and pay lower taxes and shrink government all at the same time.

This was the essence of the argument in 1980, but by 1988, government had grown considerably, adding 61,000 Federal jobs to Washington. Also, taxes were raised three times, in 1983 (gas tax), in 1984, and in the Tax Reform Act of 1986. Finally, America piled on 2.7 trillion dollars to the national debt in those eight years. The people were sold the very appealing mantra of lower taxes, smaller government and affordable defense, but that was not the reality that was delivered by Washington D.C.

"The Running Man" reflects the huge gap between reality and fantasy that we saw in real life during those years. Damon Killian – whose name always makes me think of Simon Cowell – is a character who puts on a face of love and kindness for audiences. He kisses old ladies, and hand-holds nervous contestants. But he is actually a mean-spirited, power-mad, control-freak. In one scene, Killian nearly trips on a newly waxed floor in his office building. An employee apologizes to him, and Killian graciously accepts the apology to the employee's face. As soon as the custodian is gone, Killian orders him to be fired. The face of the establishment is affable, but the actions are destructive to those not in power.

This is just one small example of the reality/imagery gap. As mentioned above, Killian has the Bakersfield food riot videotape edited so that it presents a lie, the very opposite of the truth. A man who should be lauded as a hero, Richards, is instead despised as a villain...all so Killian can get better ratings. Similarly, Killian makes another attempt to deceive audiences late in the film, utilizing "traveling mattes" and other state-of-the-art special effects techniques to make it appear as though Richards is killed in the contest when, in fact, he has escaped unharmed. The message: make people live in a constructed reality, rather than face real life. Today we call this an ideological bubble.

Another of Killian's lies: last season's winners on "The Running Man" are not celebrating on a tropical beach somewhere, they've been murdered by Killian.

Described succinctly, everything Killian does in public and for the TV show is a show. It bears no resemblance to reality. It's just show business...but this behavior is especially sinister in the film because lives are on the line, and the movie has explicitly connected show business to politics and government.

The people of America aren't exactly spared harsh criticism by this satire either. Although Killian repeatedly discusses "traditional morality" and such on "The Running Man," the people in America are actually nourished on a steady diet of violence, avarice and perversion.

We see this fact exemplified in one of the commercials made for the film, "Climbing for Dollars," which shows hungry dogs nipping at the feet of contestants as they climb a rope, scrambling to collect money.

At another point, we see a poster for a television series titled "The Hate Boat." Again, this is not traditional morality, it's sex and violence as governmental distraction or sleight-of-hand. As long as we're watching the telly, we're not watching the actions of our overlords as they dismantle democracy.

The audience members watching "The Running Man" are particularly fickle too. At first they mourn when their gladiators die in battle. But soon enough, they are hooting and hollering in favor of Richards, the very man who killed their "favorites."

Again, the projected image is one of decency and traditional values, but it's not real. "Words can't express" how sad the audience feels at the loss of their heroes says Killian. But then he cuts to commercials, and sells more "Cadre Cola."

Apparently mourning can't get in the way of making a few bucks. And the audience can't even remember who they were rooting for before the commercial break.

"The Running Man" works efficiently as a satire because it reveals so well how films and TV can, in the wrong hands, be utterly manipulated and manipulative. The film's master-stroke regarding this leitmotif involves the casting of Richard Dawson, former host of "Family Feud." Hiring Dawson was a real coup, because he very ably mocks his familiar game show persona but then layers on the screen character's private, caustic face. Dawson makes for an extraordinary villain by playing on our expectations and then totally subverting them.

In *The New York Times*, Vincent Canby noted: "Mr. Dawson, who was the host of television's long-running "Family Feud" game show, is wonderfully comic as a fellow who'd star his own beloved dad as the "running man" if it would buy him a few points. His hair always perfectly blow-dried, his haberdashery immaculate, Mr. Dawson steals the movie as a personality composed of equal parts of Phil Donahue, Merv Griffin and Maximilien Francois Marie Isidore (Mickey) Robespierre."

More than the imposing Schwarzenegger, Dawson is the fuel that drives "The Running Man," making it so very wicked, so much fun, and seemingly so real.

That established, this is also one of the Governator's most impressive film performances. *The Washington Post wrote:* "Pumped and primed for self-parody, the burly star proves as funny as he is ferocious in this tough guy's commentary on America's preoccupation with violence and game shows." I agree with that review as well. If Dawson is willing to mock his public image here (and he is), Schwarzenegger courageously goes down that same path with his co-star, even mimicking his most famous screen line, "I'll be back," and opening himself up for Dawson's great comeback.

"Only in reruns..."

There's something very post-modern happening here. "The Running Man" tackles the unholy juncture of television and politics at the same time that it playfully pivots off our intimate knowledge and affection for Dawson's and Schwarzenegger's familiar screen personas. It's a very, very...meta equation, for lack of a better term.

I only wish that the action scenes in "The Running Man" were a little more varied, a little less predictable. A killer is called on stage, and then he goes in to hunt Richards. Richard is victorious and it's time for another hunter. Rinse and repeat. Watching the film, you get the distinct sense that all of the talent was energized by the film's witty ideas, but that the action scenes were sort of left to fend for themselves. Of course, as I noted above, the repetitive nature of the fight scenes could be a deliberate allusion to the repetitive nature of game shows. We tune in every week to see the same thing, don't we?

Still, "The Running Man" isn't out of steam, even today. It gets a lot of the "future" detail just right. From fears of an economic collapse to fuel shortages, the film makes some pretty accurate guesses about the 2010s. At one point, Ben Richards books his escape route/

travel itinerary on an interactive television set, a precursor to something we do on the Internet now all the time.

And also, of course, this 1987 film seems to understand that our television and politics were headed towards a generation of ingrained and unimaginable cruelty.

It's not a pretty picture, but I bet that with just a few tweaks here and there, Killian's "The Running Man" would be a pretty big hit these days....

Cult-Movie Review: The Blood of Heroes (1989)

(By John Kenneth Muir Copyright ©John Kenneth Muir)

"The Blood of Heroes" (1989) – a film concerning a particularly vicious sport called "Jugger"– is one of my favorite, under-recognized genre movies of the late eighties.

Ever since I first saw "Rollerball" (1975), I have been fascinated with the future of professional sports. We know that professional sports will likely remain extremely commercial and profitable going forward, but we also know today that some are becoming more brutal, and that concussions and brain damage are often the unfortunate result for some football players.

Not exactly a "good sport" is it, when competitors end up with catastrophic brain injuries...

Regardless, "The Blood of Heroes" is a violent and enthralling post-apocalyptic film. In some senses, it's actually the "Rocky" (1976) of the dystopia genre, because it gets the audience squarely behind its underdog heroes, and resolves in an incredibly hard-fought victory, with the heroic athletes bloodied but unbroken.

Unusually, the film is also a rite-of-passage story with a strong female character, Joan Chen's Kidda, holding center stage. Most often, even in today's cinema, the hero's journey is a male one, but Kidda and her dreams of a better life pulsate at the heart of the film's action. Rutger Hauer portrays an experienced Jugger player named Sallow, but in many ways, this veteran actor takes on the supporting role of the "wise elder," revealing to Kidda the ropes of the game, and, importantly, the politics behind the game.

Reviews for "The Blood of Heroes" were mixed upon theatrical release. Vincent Canby at *The New York Times* championed the film and wrote that it is "entertainingly grim and, in an upside-down way, romantic."

Time-Out, meanwhile, noted that The Blood of Heroes (a.k.a. The Salute of the Jugger) offered "little to look at and nothing worth hearing."

In this instance, I agree with Canby's conclusion.

Although characterization in the film is ultimately subordinate to the frequent and violent jugger matches, one nevertheless develops genuine affection for the players here: Hauer, Chen, Vincent D'Onofrio and Delroy Lindo.

And although it is easy to gaze at the film and conclude that the narrative is somewhat meandering or plot-less, this episodic quality, this loose structure, actually works in the film's favor. Watching "The Blood of Heroes," you are afforded a real taste of the Jugger's life, from the wearying nomadic existence, to the violence and intensity of the sport, to the seemingly-endless ritual of tending to wounds and bruises after a match. The film repeats this sequence of events over and over, until you feel like you're right there with the athletes, sweating and bleeding alongside them.

Perhaps "The Blood of Heroes'" underlying message isn't entirely deep, but it is nevertheless worthwhile. The film suggests we are all tougher than we think, and that even when the forces of the world seem aligned against us, we'll keep fighting and striving for something better than the status quo.

"Play hard, you'll forget the fear."

"The Blood of Heroes" is set in a post-apocalyptic world in which (most) folks no longer have the time or luxury to think about professional sports, at least as we understand them now. The world's infrastructure has collapsed following a series of wars, and folks no longer remember the "Golden Age of the 20th century" or "the miraculous technology or cruel wars that followed."

Accordingly, the popular game of Jugger removes the commercialism and professionalism of modern-day sports, but amps up the brutality angle. In this violent game, a team consisting of several players – a "qwik," a "chain," an "enforcer" and a "slicer" – battles an opposing team. The match is bloody and violent, and doesn't end until the winning team manages to place a dog skull on a pike, or stake. Roving Jugger teams subsist by beating local teams, and collecting tributes for their victories.

The film follows a group of nomadic players, led by taciturn Sallow (Hauer). His team comes upon a farming community where a passionate young woman, Kidda (Chen), wants to join the team as "qwik." Kidda boasts dreams of playing in "the League," inside one of the nine cities. Sallow himself was once in "the League" but was expelled from high society for his inappropriate behavior with a lord's concubine. Since that time, Sallow has eschewed contact with the cities, but he nonetheless tells Kidda a challenge can be issued to the city's team. If the team accepts…they're in!

After several victories, Sallow's team travels to a city to mount such a challenge, but the wronged Lord – named Vile – still wants Sallow punished and humiliated. He instructs the city's team leader, Gonzo, to blind Sallow during the match, and then, essentially, to beat him to a pulp.

The match in the city commences in bloody fashion, and for Kidda and Sallow, their future is on the line…

"Juggers can't fuck after the game. It doesn't work. Unless you like to rub wounds against wounds."

In the introduction to this review, I mentioned "Rocky" as a clear antecedent to "The Blood of Heroes," but perhaps, in terms of sports movies, I also should have made notation of "Bull Durham" (1987) too. In that classic baseball movie – one of the best ever made – a player named Crash (Kevin Costner) is cast out of the minor leagues and sent down to the Single A division to mentor a promising player, one who could make it all the way to the majors. As that player rises, Crash hopes to rise again too…

In very, very broad strokes, "The Blood of Heroes" follows a similar sort of outline, with an aging player, tossed from the big leagues, coming to mentor a young, promising player in a smaller, less professional venue. Sallow and Kidda represent those characters here, but in both situations there's this the idea of a cycle: of the old, wiser player not only tutoring the young, but returning to the world that, at some point, wronged him. In terms of visuals, "The Blood of Heroes," written and directed by David Peoples, clearly owes a lot to "The Road Warrior" (1982) aesthetic, and yet thematically it is much more a sports movie than a science fiction epic.

Here – as in real life – athletic prowess is one of the few ways one can successfully bridge the gap in an unequal economic system. In the film, we see the immaculately-dressed, immaculately-cleaned upper class citizens of the underground city, and can contrast their aristocratic look with that of the Juggers, who are leathery, filthy, wind-blown, and marred by scars and bruises. Just as is the case in our society, the upper classes are willing to pay handsomely to be entertained by good athletes, and thus a sense of class warfare seems present in all interactions. One upper-class woman likes to decorate her porcelain skin with the blood of Jugger players, and so there's also an impression of a vampire-like over-class lording it over the under-class.

Uniquely, at its valedictory moment, "The Blood of Heroes" visually mirrors to its spiritual cinematic antecedent, the aforementioned "Rollerball." There, in the final battle, James Caan's player Jonathan E defeated the last enemy player right in front of his nemesis, an executive played by John Houseman. Specifically, he checked the opposing player into the glass barrier separating him from Houseman.

Here, director Peoples' stages a nearly identical shot, with Sallow taking out Gonzo, just inches from Vile, in front of Vile's box seats (behind a kind of protective cage).

In both cases the same idea is transmitted: the notion of individualism trumping established order, or authority.

In both cases, defiance beats obedience.

If anything at all undercuts the success of "The Blood of Heroes," it is the final triumphal note the film sounds after Sallow and Kidda win the day. Immediately, the vulture-like upper class descends upon them, congratulating the players, flirting with them, chatting them up. The implication is that Sallow, Kidda and the others are now in like flint, and welcomed into a life of comfort and luxury.

But really, aren't these Jugger players letting the establishment absorb them, at this point, and becoming part of the corrupt 1% percent in the process? Aren't they, by joining the league, playing the aristocracy's game? I like some of the early shots set in the city, where Sallow and Kidda are literally on the outside looking in (through bars on the windows) at the upper class, but the ending seems to undercut this crucial sense of outsider-ism.

It seems that the real point of the movie is (or should be...) that reaching the top doesn't necessarily put you where you want to be.

Once you get there, you realize you're still trapped playing another man's sport.

Aside from that complaint, "The Blood of Heroes" is a rousing sports movie in a dystopian setting. Shot in Australia, the film makes the most of its picturesque exteriors, and we see every variation of jugger match known to man. The game is played in the scorching sun, and in the rain and mud. There's also some interesting symbolism in the film in the form of the game itself: a literalization of the notion of picking over the bones of a dead world. That's what Jugger is, literally, a battle to win a skull, a bone...something dead and useless.

"The Blood of Heroes" is a visceral and involving film, in my judgment, and one made doubly so by the twin decisions to keep dialogue to a minimum and to not over-burden the narrative with more incident or detail than necessary. As I wrote above, the film is extremely episodic and repetitive: travel, play, sew up wounds. Rinse and repeat. If you allow yourself to go with the flow, you can fall into synch with the movie's distinctive, almost-trance-like rhythm and literally almost feel what it's like to dwell in this world of sweat, dirt and blood.

And given the alternative of those porcelain-skinned, aristocratic vampires, you may even come to agree with Sallow's opinion that scarred skin – like this violent but memorable film – is strangely beautiful in its own way.

Revisiting The Blood of Heroes AKA Salute of the Jugger

(By Eion Friel Copyright ©Eion Friel)

I've always loved low budget post-apocalyptic movies from the 80's and 90s; it doesn't matter how cheap they are as it just makes it more effective as if it's like documentary footage.

"The Blood of Heroes" AKA "The Salute of the Jugger" doesn't have a massive budget lacking special effects or big set-pieces but that makes it feel more real as the world in this movie is without technology where a group of "Juggers" travelling the landscape partake in a violent sport involving a dog skull. The movie basically consists of everyone beating the living Hell out of each other for this sport with a few character moments in between.

Joan Chen is the ambitious player Kidda who joins Sallow (Rutger Hauer) and his crew as they battle their way to the leagues; I've got to hand it to Chen, she really wasn't afraid to do a lot of physical work for this movie and it looks like everyone was getting genuinely injured. This film is also notable for early performances from Vincent D'Onofrio (who I just met last weekend) and Delroy Lindo who are part of Sallow's team.

Hauer is at his stoic best in this movie with Sallow generally showing little emotion; however, as the film progresses we realize he wants nothing more than to rejoin the leagues and feel like a winner again. I found myself caring for these characters and really wanted them to succeed in this harsh world.

I was reading a review for this film on IMDb by someone who worked on it and the final version was apparently cut to ribbons with some interesting scenes removed. There are still alternate versions of the film with the US edition coming in 10 minutes shorter than the international version; in 2017 a 2 disc Blu-ray was released of the film in Japan but I hope a boutique Blu-ray company in North America can give us a new remastered release with the alternate versions of the film.

Overall, "Salute of the Jugger" AKA "The Blood of Heroes" is an entertaining post-apocalyptic adventure with solid performances from the entire cast with Joan Chen a particular standout as the ambitious Kidda. Rutger Hauer is hard as nails showing little emotion but we root for him anyway due to his sheer charisma. The sport itself is a fascinating creation and makes for brutal entertainment.

The Sporting Allegory: Decoding the Mystery of Jugger's Greeting and Quintet's Harmony

"Salute the Jugger" is a story about survival in a post-apocalyptic world. In the futuristic society of these stories the downtrodden masses find relief and escape via a brutal game called "The Game." Like films "Mad Max: Beyond Thunderdome" and "Rollerball," "The Game" is similarly a metaphor for the relentless fight for existence in a society where survival is a tough dream.

This movie just showcases the use of symbols of power, regime, and human experience in the midst of events. The character Sallow, played by Rutger Hauer, represents the character that is ethically gray, the one that we usually see in movies like this. He has to face the demons and struggles through the chaos and disorder of the world. For Joan's character, Kidda, determination, and hope are indispensable qualities that make her survive in a world that is filled with obstacles. Inspired by her tough experiences and regrets, she strives to find redemption.

The difference of "Salute of the Jugger" from traditional movies in the way of style is the way it approaches personalities and explores in a very realistic and complex way. Instead of beautiful choreography of actions from "Mad Max" or a luminous display of dystopia in "Rollerball," "Salute of the Jugger" tracks individuals and goes deeper into the reasons behind their choices.

To some extent "Salute of the Jugger" and "Quintet" have common characteristics. They both employ the prowess of sports to reflect on the difficulties associated with the fight for existence in the post-apocalyptic world. Despite their differences, at a closer look you can clearly see how both motion pictures portray the gritty realities of their supposed universes through gaming. Moreover, these themes reflect the impact of popularity addiction on society and the patterns of entertainment of sports. These representations force us to raise this passing question if succeeding in popularity matters, or the chase of splendor serves the life purpose.

Although "Salute of the Jugger" and "Quintet" differ from each other significantly as they deal with the style and the sporting events instead, they are able to connect on the main motif of using the games as a symbol of struggle in the people's existence. Through displaying games these films let us experience the challenging situations of these personalities and teach us some important lessons about our existence in the midst of chaos and hopelessness. These films withstand the sands of time as in "Salute of the Jugger" and "Quintet" provide thrills with their enthralling themes and captivating stories.

The Brutal Intersection of Sport and Survival: Let us turn to Salute of the Jugger and Mad Max: Beyond Thunderdome

In a dystopian society, both "The Jugger" and "Mad Max: Beyond Thunderdome" examine the issue of how sports can easily become the fastest way of surviving. In these dark worlds, sports become a process for those with power to make sure they remain in charge and fixate on themselves, while the oppressed consider it as a way to regain their lost humanity and stand up against the oppressive regimes. The characters in the movies are the protagonists of a vicious competition, not only to survive or to exercise their power but also to define their identity. In the course of their struggle, their will and strength are able to find that tiny spark of hope and atonement which seemed to have vanished from the world completely.

The people form bonds of teamwork as they put their heads together and work to achieve what at first seemed unachievable. Through their efforts, these associations show tenacity and steadfastness even in an environment that seems to have no hope, bringing a glimmer of the belief as to what will happen in the future.

"The Salute of the Jugger" and "Mad Max: Beyond Thunderdome" apply the principle of sport to explore the themes of oppression and resistance, community and solidarity in a post-apocalyptic world. Through these movies, the power of human spirit is emphasized in the most challenging situations, which provides hope and a glimmer of a much brighter tomorrow.

Discovering the Gritty Realism of Apocalyptic Fiction: Salute the Jugger and its Commonality with the Genre

"Salute of the Jugger" is for sure a jewel in the crown of dystopian cinematography. It is directed by David Webb Peoples and the actors Rutger Hauer and Joan Chen are the featured artists that bring the movie back to life with styles on survival, redemption, and humanity that is extremely strong in a world devastated by an apocalypse. Whilst it might not get the level of regard as "Mad Max" or "Rollerball," "Salute to the Jugger" presents a raw and original depiction of life in a desert landscape in which are still comparable central ideas.

The story is about the struggle for existence, death being the only alternative, against such impossible odds, in a backdrop of a post-apocalyptic world – when cultures and civilizations have collapsed. "The Game" that is being lived on this planet becomes not only entertainment but also a glimpse of hope for the people who stand on the brink of survival. It literally portrays individuals struggling to live in a negative environment of the world without any positive reflection or empathy.

The narrative of "The Salute to the Jugger," however, touches on the notion of power inequality, control, and human resilience irrespective of the environmental conditions. Rutger Hauer does a great job playing the role of Sallow, an anti-hero who we usually see in films of this category. While Joan Chen perfectly depicts Kidda, a kindred spirit.

The film is a captivating one with its striking visuals, subtle and powerful dialogs and haunting soundtrack. You are completely engulfed in the cruel and unrepentant world. It gives the feeling of stress and credibility that doesn't go away even after the enjoyment is over. A highlight of "Salute of the Jugger" that makes it stand out from similar films is its genuine and finely drawn portrayal of the personalities and their individual problems. The movie just doesn't deal with the storyline; it also digs deep into the human drama and emotional complexities of the story.

Although "Salute of the Jugger" did not gain much recognition as similar apocalyptic and dystopian movies, it definitely has its importance and impact. This film being a symbol of the power invigorating with the stories which draw people in with different moods and shows the unrestricted view of life in a destroyed world. However, though it may not have received a lot of attention in comparison to other apocalyptic and dystopian movies, "Salute of the Jugger" emerges as an exceptional exemplification of the strength of storytelling, an ability to shake the world through emotions and a truly dramatic manifestation of our lives in a broken planet.

PKD predates 'Terminator' with 'Vulcan's Hammer' (1960)

(By John Hansen Copyright © John Hansen https://
reviewsfrommycouch.com/)

"Vulcan's Hammer" (written in 1953, published in 1960) is Philip K. Dick's first foray into novel-length science fiction (although not his first published), and it's a difficult book to judge. Its warning about a government handing power to a supercomputer is today an SF staple, with the entire "Terminator" franchise built around it.

But at the time of its writing, it was more eye-opening. And obviously the theme of rational but cruel artificial intelligence was fascinating to Dick, who went on to rework and remold this concept many times.

Short and fast-moving

"Vulcan's Hammer" is short and fast-moving. This is to its detriment in a way, since bureaucrat William Barris flies back and forth from New York (his territory) to Geneva (Earth's capital) so many times that it's mind-spinning. Granted, PKD's point is probably that future plane travel (or flying "ship" travel, as it were) is fast and easy.

But the climactic battle where the forces of good take on the supercomputer Vulcan 3 is logistically ridiculous, with soldiers being as easy for bureaucrats to utilize as pawns on a chess board. As such, PKD is unable to stick the landing, a problem similar to another early novel, "The Cosmic Puppets."

I don't know if PKD intended this, but "Vulcan's Hammer" can be read as an argument that bureaucrats are people too, despite the fact that the novel is unquestionably a cautionary tale against big governments. This novel features the biggest of all possible governments; it's worldwide and it's brutal in its pursuit of an ideal that is also its name: Unity.

Barris exists within the system that rewards power grabs and internal connections, but PKD sympathizes with him. Partially it's because he's the POV character, and readers will always go easy on the person we're in the trenches with. But partially, the author really does give him sympathetic (if undercooked) qualities, including Barris being good at his job and his admirable stance of never siding with killers.

As the story moves forward, Unity members are faced with the binary choice of siding with Vulcan 3 (the supercomputer leader of Unity) or the Healers (the resistance). Barris declines to side with the Healers, noting that they are killers.

Skimming over some horrors

While I admire his idealism, and his rejection of the false binary choice, it should be noted that PKD skims over something that must be a reality of this world: that Unity stays in power through ruthless means. Totalitarian governments are by definition ruthless. The only way they wouldn't be is if no one desired freedom and was fine with having their lives mapped out for them, and that's clearly not the case here.

That flaw aside, PKD makes several good socio-political observations throughout "Vulcan's Hammer," including schools as indoctrination centers, politics as an exercise in power-holding rather than societal improvement, the way socialism fixes the size of the pie and encourages backstabbing rather than cooperation, a government job as a path to financial success, and freedom as an innate human desire that goes beyond economic status.

He also starts thinking about how people can make the wrong decision because they misunderstand what's missing from the information available to them; this would later be the centerpiece and twist of the short story "The Minority Report." Vulcan 2, Vulcan 3 and the most powerful man in Unity, Jason Dill, all make decisions without knowing every piece of information.

They know information is being withheld by another entity, but they misunderstand the meaning of that. There's some convoluted "He doesn't know that I know he thinks I don't know" logic (or false logic) at play here.

2029 feels a lot like 1960

PKD does his usual SF writing exercise, common in these early novels, where he moves society's present-day (of his writing) behavior into the future (this story is set in 2029; I'm not sure if "The Terminator" was paying homage by also using this date for its Future War), but the only change is futuristic technology. So it comes off as a satire. But really, PKD is just writing down his observations about how big governments operate.

PKD tries a little too hard with the technology predictions, so we get his staple underestimation of the future wherein characters feed cards into computers to communicate with them. He would have been better off portraying human-computer interactions as something that just happens, something that's almost magical. That's how people understand the internet today, anyway.

He almost strikes comedy gold with the Hammers, which stand in for modern war drones, but overall "Vulcan's Hammer" isn't as crazily funny as the best PKD works. The book's warnings are not only old hat in a world where a sixth "Terminator" film was recently released, but they are presented in sober, straightforward fashion.

But PKD's theme of bloated and liberty-quashing governments is valid and always will be, so it's by no means a waste of 163 pages to dig into it.

'12 Monkeys' (1995) is a stylish, confusing take on time travel

(By John Hansen Copyright © John Hansen
https://reviewsfrommycouch.com/)

A dystopian 2035

Based on a short French film by Chris Marker, "12 Monkeys" is not about monkeys starting a pandemic (that's "Outbreak"). It's hard to know right away what it's about, other than the crappy conditions of 2035, where Bruce Willis' James Cole and other prisoners of the state "live like worms." Nonetheless, "12 Monkeys" is watchable because of Willis' sympathetic turn, one of the best of his career. As a reluctant time-traveling investigator, he has great chemistry with Madeleine Stowe's Dr. Kate Railly.

Loosely speaking, this is the "Terminator" time-travel situation wherein Cole has to convince Kate he's from the future and has to take important steps. But it's more complex than that in both good and bad ways. The screenplay sometimes creates artificial confusion. For example, we see Cole go through the time-traveling process the second time he goes back in time. Why not show the process before the first trip? There's no good reason, other than to play coy with the audience.

That said, the way the film looks at time travel is rather original. For one thing, the times Cole travels back to – 1990 (by mistake), the 1800s (by mistake) and 1996 (on purpose) – are The Past. 2035 is The Present. When you're in The Past, you can learn information; indeed, it's Cole's mission to learn the source of the deadly virus. That will be the first step in allowing humans to repopulate the virus-laden surface in 2035. But you can't change anything in The Past.

Additionally, the human brain is not meant to withstand all this time travel. So we get a rare situation where Cole thinks he's crazy and Kate – who has seen Cole wink out of existence when he's pulled back by his handlers in 2035 – has to convince him he's sane.

Information-gathering mission

I can't say they didn't warn me, as this is indeed an information-gathering mission, but the ending is rather flat, with Cole learning the actual source of the virus. In retrospect, most of the film finds him chasing a red herring. While a lot of discussion about "12 Monkeys" centers on the question of what exactly happens (those YouTube "Explained" videos are made for movies like this), one could also ask what the meaning of the film is.

While it's a neat twist that young Cole sees his future self – as well as his future lover, Kate — in an airport in 1996, there's no emotional or insightful point to it. And there are whole stretches of this film that could have been condensed without hurting the narrative – notably the psych-ward sequence where Cole meets Brad Pitt's Jeffrey Goines.

Pitt chews scenery, but I was more impressed with Willis' turn in this rare role where he runs the gamut of feelings. Cole is totally put-upon in the future, where he has no choice but to go on this mission that will probably kill him. And yes, he has the Cassandra Complex of dealing with people who won't believe he's a time-traveler.

But I love it when he smiles in childlike fashion, marveling at fresh air and the radio, noting that "the 20th century had the best music." We can see why Kate is won over by this man who kidnapped her; it's not a case of Stockholm Syndrome. As unkind as its view of people is, "12 Monkeys" makes a case for humanity through Cole and Kate.

Designing a bleak future

The production design by Jeffrey Beecroft ("A Quiet Place") drives home the point of how unappealing a post-virus future could be. When Cole is being instructed or debriefed by the 2035 scientist-rulers, he's on a chair high up on a wall. Despite this, he is in the weaker position because a menacing bank of TV monitors floats nearby, with the scientists represented by close-ups of an eye.

The Big Brother state, wherein people are plucked with a giant hook from their hovel-cages whenever the scientists or foremen need them, is the least of it. The surface is covered in snow and grizzly bears, and if your suit punctures, you're dead. But the most poignant depiction of a sad future comes when we see a clean department store in 1996 and Cole has a mind-flash of the store's ruins in 2035.

"12 Monkeys" is too in love with its artificial twists and turns, and it spends too much time in the nuthouse showing off Pitt's performance. Still, even as the narrative meanders away from the search for the virus' origin, the production design and a game Bruce Willis are nothing to sneeze at.

The Postman - From Novel To Movie

"The Postman," a novel written by David Brin, is situated in a post-apocalyptic world, providing an insight into a dystopian society. The narrative depicts a solitary character who ventures through the desolate landscapes of Oregon, discovering a uniform worn by the United States Postal Service personnel. Adorning the outfit, the protagonist assumes the task of a postman and declares himself as a federal inspector representing the recently re-established "Restored United States of America." By performing his duties and asserting the resurgence of a central government, he instills optimism in a populace endangered by an authoritarian militia with tendencies toward the neo-feudal.

Dave Langford reviewed "The Postman" for White Dwarf #83, and stated that "The story is complicated by Krantz's intersection with another myth in the making, and then by a muddle of battle, murder and enhanced super-guerillas, all a bit of a needless distraction, but never mind. It's nicely written, sometimes moving, and ends as it should. Well worth reading."[172]

Released as a movie in 1997, "The Postman" is an American epic post-apocalyptic adventure film helmed by Kevin Costner, who also takes on the lead role. Eric Roth and Brian Helgeland adapted the screenplay from David Brin's 1985 novel of the same title. As well as Costner, the movie stars Will Patton, Larenz Tate, Olivia Williams, James Russo, and Tom Petty.

Although the film was a box-office bomb, only grossing $20.8 million worldwide against a budget of $80 million, it was nominated for three Saturn Awards. However, it won all five of its Golden Raspberry Award nominations, including Worst Picture. Over time, the film has gained a cult following and has been better received.

---

[172] *Dave Langford (November 1986). "Critical Mass." White Dwarf. Games Workshop (83): 8.*

Critical Reviews of The Postman:

Todd McCarthy, *Variety*: "The sweeping movement of the tale across half a continent, and the frequent action that facilitates it, is conveyed in a majestic and for the most part exciting manner."[173]

Frederic and Mary Ann Brussat, Spirituality & Practice: "Emblazons hope as a powerful spiritual force."[174]

John R. McEwen, Film Quips Online: "Stephen F. Windon's cinematography is at times astounding, and there is good acting by Costner, Olivia Williams as his girlfriend, and Will Patton as General Bethlehem, the Holnist leader. Also notable is Larenz Tate as Costner's overzealous first recruit in the Postal army."[175]

Nicole Bartner, Denofgeek.com: "The Postman has heightened relevance in the Post 9/11 era because it is offering an object lesson in what I believe is true about Americans now: 9/11 could not happen again because Americans will simply not sit by on a plane and allow it to happen."[176]

Kevin Costner on the film: "You know, I thought it was a pretty funny movie set against the idea of a Superman — somebody stepping up. But in this case, it's a very humble guy who's nothing but a liar [laughs] — delivers mail and burns half of it just to stay alive. So, I like the movie."[177]

In an interview with Metro before filming began, author David Brin said that, unlike typical post-apocalyptic movies that satisfy "little-boy wish fantasies about running amok in a world without rules," the intended moral of "The Postman" is that "if we lost our civilization, we'd all come to realize how much we missed it, and

---

[173] *Todd McCarthy, Variety (Dec 16, 1997)*

[174] *Frederic and Mary Ann Brussat, Spirituality & Practice (Mar 1, 2002)*

[175] *John R. McEwen, Film Quips Onlinehttp://www.filmquipsonline.com/postman.html*

[176] *Nicole Bartner, Denofgeek.com (Oct 18, 2012)*

[177] *Mike Ryan (June 5, 2013). "Kevin Costner, 'Man of Steel' Star, Looks Back on 'Bull Durham,' 'Waterworld' and the First Time He Made a Million Dollars." HuffPost.*

would realize what a miracle it is simply to get your mail every day."[178]

---

[178] *Zack Stentz (June 12, 1997), "Brin on science fiction, society and Kevin Costner,"*
Metro.

Delivering The Mail with The Postman: An Interview with First Assistant Director - Dennis Maguire

Q: How did you get involved with The Postman?

A: I received a call for an interview, which was surprising because I was not familiar with Kevin Costner, his producing partner Jim Wilson, or the production. However, I went in for the interview with Kevin and Jim, thinking it was interesting. I read the script, which was epic and knew it would be a challenging shoot because it was very long. The first draft I read was 159 pages, which is much longer than typical screenplays that are around 119 pages. I assumed there would be cuts, but there weren't. Although no one explicitly told me, I think the vice president of production, Bill Young, who was very kind to me, may have recommended me for the project. However, I didn't realize this until years later. It's been almost 30 years since I worked on the film. I was hired and hit the ground running because the previous person who had worked on Dances with Wolves may have been involved; but didn't end up doing it. I heard rumors about the reasons why, but you never really know. Our DP, Stephen Windon, was an experienced Australian operator, but Warner Brothers was initially skeptical about giving the massive show to a first-timer Director of Photography. They wanted someone who could help guide the picture, especially considering Kevin's previous films that ran over schedule.

Q: How did you work with the filmmakers on set?

A: As the first assistant director, I was actively involved in every department because Kevin was not always available during prep of the film. We originally thought about shooting digital and even did a test day with the Sony digital camera at Jim Wilson's ranch in Calabasas, California. We shot side by side film and digital and then held a big screening with Warner Brothers executives. Ultimately, the decision was made to shoot film due to the ambitious nature of the project, which involved shooting in four different states with adverse weather and shooting conditions. While I did bring up concerns about the length of the script and the 100-day schedule with Kevin Costner and Jim Wilson, Kevin was adamant about keeping the script as is. As the assistant director, it was not my job to make those decisions, and we ended up shooting for 118 days across multiple states. While it was a challenging shoot, I was thankful to have received recognition from Terry Semel, Bob Daley, and Lorenzo di Bonaventura for bringing the picture on schedule and budget in their mind; although we were not on either account.

Q: What memories do you have of the cast and crew?

A: I thought the cast was excellent. The large ensemble included many actor friends, family members, with many having smaller roles. Overall, the young actors were fantastic, but I recall a situation where we were filming a town scene and many of them were idle and uninvolved. As the 1st assistant director, I spoke with them and encouraged them to participate, explaining that even if they weren't directly in the scene, they were still a part of the film and could contribute by creating improvised scenes and interactions. I reminded them that screen time was valuable and that they should take advantage of any opportunity to be involved. Some of them took my advice and began interacting and creating vignettes on set. Even the director, Kevin, got involved and provided guidance for their work. One of the young actors thanked me afterward, and I explained that we were all a team and that being involved and present on set was essential. Likewise, communication among the various departments was crucial, with efficient assistant directors ensuring that everyone was informed and working toward the same goal. This was something that I had learned and experienced throughout my career, and it helped to make productions run smoothly and successfully.

Q: What are your favorite memories of working on this production?

A: It was an epic experience. The project was massive, and I felt the pressure to deliver. [without script approval from the director.] I had a meeting with Jim Wilson and suggested that we have everything there on set since the director didn't have time to go through the script page by page. We had to have a crane and other pieces of equipment with us at all times because we were so remote from equipment houses. Which was expensive, but I knew we needed it due to the crane work required based on what I had heard and from my viewing of Dances with Wolves. Every day, we had to create on the spot, and some of those days were pretty epic. We shot in the copper mine outside of Tucson, Arizona, where we had built a massive 'wholeness' camp. We had 250 re-enactors who generally re-enact Civil War battles, dressed up as 'wholeness soldiers' for battle scenes.

It was a big deal for the re-enactors, who brought their motorhomes, caravans, and tents to the set and lived there in all 4 states we filmed in. We fed and treated the horses, had proper shower, bathroom facilities, and meals, which they cooked themselves. They were paid for the day and even had a veterinarian on call. I remembered seeing them dressed up as Mujahideen on Rambo III in the 80s, and now they were dressed up as 'wholeness soldiers.'

It was fun to see Kevin watching the re-enactors in formation, as they recognized me. Some of them were from Rambo III, and Kevin was a little jealous that they all knew me. We had many unique shooting locations, including Bend, Oregon, which provided beautiful scenery.

Q: Have you read the novel The Postman by David Brin?

A: No, I haven't. I knew it was a book, and I knew that Dick Donner had tried to make it into a film. So I spoke to his first assistant and producer, Jim Van Wyck, who is now retired. His son-in-law, Jayson Merrill, was also my second assistant director at the time, and he's currently a very successful first assistant director. Jimmy told me that they had considered working on the project, did some preliminary budgeting, scouting, and discussed art direction. Ultimately, Dick Donner decided not to pursue it with Warner Brothers. Years later, the project was passed on to Kevin. During the early stages of pre-production, I had difficulty meeting with Kevin because he was frequently unavailable and often out of town. Additionally, Kevin's production designer, Ida Random, who was an older woman with notable credits, had been on the project for months prior to my involvement, but had not made much progress. When I came on board, I realized how little had been accomplished. For example, we had not completed scouting prior to our Tech Scout, which is when the department heads visit the locations for the last time before shooting begins. Since we were filming in four different states, Kevin arranged for Warner Brothers to lend us their Gulfstream 5 jet, as it could accommodate the entire crew (around 25 people). Commercial flights would have been a logistical nightmare with the crew scattered across four states, so having the private jet was a huge help in sticking to our Tech Scout schedule. However, even with the jet at our disposal, we still had not secured all the locations for shooting. Therefore, we conducted "cold scouting," where we would leave the crew on the plane and drive around looking for suitable locations. When we found a location, my staff would inform everyone and have them transported to the site in vans. It was a chaotic process, and at times I worried it would be the biggest disaster of a film I had ever been involved with. However, somehow we managed to pull it off. It was especially tough for Steve Wyndham, who didn't have much time with Kevin either. He was stressed, but I reassured him that we would get through it together. I told him to let me know if he heard anything from Kevin that I should be aware of. We did have a second unit with their own scheduled work. One time, Kevin showed up when we were shooting a sequence with the big orange 76 ball from the gas station, which was a well-known brand at the time, gas station in the United States. Instead of bringing in additional camera crews, I suggested using the second unit's cameras and crew to assist us. After we finished shooting with Kevin, they could then continue with their scheduled work, which included stunts and scenes with Kevin's double. Everyone agreed it was a good idea, and we went ahead with the plan. There were instances when Kevin showed up late or seemed unprepared, such as when he wanted to shoot a scene on top of the gas station without prior planning. Despite these challenges, we managed to make progress and shoot the necessary scenes. It was always interesting and unpredictable, but with my knowledge of filmmaking and the script, I tried to anticipate what would happen each day and keep everyone on track.

Q: What was your response to the film?

A: Overall, I was proud of the film despite the challenges we faced during the 118-day schedule. One of my biggest allies on the shoot was our Art Director, Derek Hill. The two of us always met on a new set at least one to two hours prior to crew call to make sure it was what Kevin wanted. We accomplished a great deal. During pre-production, numerous visual effects meetings took place, at least three or four, without Kevin's involvement. As a part of the production team, my goal was to make decisions that would benefit the director, his vision, the film, and the producer.

What a Wonderful World: The Dystopias of Terry Gilliam

Terry Gilliam in Sweden talking about his movie "Brazil."[60]

Terry Gilliam is a film director, screenwriter, animator, and actor who was originally from the United States. He was born on November 22, 1940, in Minneapolis, Minnesota. Gilliam has a distinct and inventive filmmaking style that often incorporates surreal and fantastical elements in his works. Although he gained recognition as a member of the Monty Python comedy troupe, contributing animations and appearing in sketches, he is predominantly renowned as a film director. Some of his most notable directorial ventures include "Brazil" (1985), "The Fisher King" (1991), "12 Monkeys" (1995), and "Fear and Loathing in Las Vegas" (1998).

Through the trilogy of films that includes "Brazil," "Twelve Monkeys," and "The Zero Theorem," Gilliam's unique blend of creative eccentricity has produced a captivating introduction to the dystopian genre.

Critical Reviews of Brazil

James Berardinelli, ReelViews:"Brazil is a stinging, Strangelovian satire of the power of the bureaucracy in an Orwellian landscape."[179]

Mike Massie, Gone with the Twins: "An uproarious satire of bureaucracy, technology, society, and humanity that proves to be one of the greatest movies of all time, sci-fi or otherwise."[180]

R.L. Shaffer, IGN DVD: "An energetically quirky social metaphor, political commentary and action/sci-fi farce all balled up into one outrageously enjoyable experience, provided you like the work of Terry Gilliam."[181]

Emanuel Levy, EmanuelLevy.Com:"Influenced by Kafka, Orwell, and Kubrick, Gilliam's darkly humorous futuristic satire is narratively flawed and excessive in many ways, but it displays its creator's wildly vivid imagination and is intermittently witty."[182]

"Brazil came specifically from the time, from the approaching of 1984. It was looming. In fact, the original title of Brazil was 1984 ½. Fellini was one of my great gods and it was 1984, so let's put them together. Unfortunately, that bastard Michael Radford did a version of 1984 and he called it 1984, so I was blown."—**Terry Gilliam**[183]

Critical Reviews of Twelve Monkeys

Jonathan Rosenbaum, *Chicago Reader*: "While all of Gilliam's movies are worth seeing, there's a fair amount of his designer grimness here mixed in with the cabaret comedy."[184]

---

179 *https://www.reelviews.net/reelviews/brazil*

180 *https://gonewiththetwins.com/new/brazil-1985/*

181 *https://www.ign.com/articles/2011/07/11/brazil-blu-ray-review*

182 *Emanuel Levy EmanuelLevy.Com (April 10, 2009).*

183 *"Salman Rushdie talks with Terry Gilliam". The Believer. Las Vegas, Nevada: University of Nevada, Las Vegas. 1 (1). March 2003.*

184 *https://chicagoreader.com/chicago/12-monkeys/Film/?oid=1054906*

Geoff Andrew, Time Out: "Gilliam gives the material a lunatic poetry of his own, but remains impervious to the requirements of narrative pacing."[185]

Ed Potton, *Times* (UK): "This dystopian time-travelling sci-fi is a reminder that the director can make films that are visually inventive, intellectually engaging and downright exciting."[186]

Janet Maslin, *New York Times*: "There's always overripe method to his madness, but in the new 12 Monkeys Mr. Gilliam's methods are uncommonly wrenching and strong."[187]

"Cole has been thrust from another world into ours and he's confronted by the confusion we live in, which most people somehow accept as normal. So he appears abnormal, and what's happening around him seems random and weird. Is he mad or are we?" **—Terry Gilliam on Twelve Monkeys lead character played by Bruce Willis[188]**

Filmmakers Keith Fulton and Louis Pepe chronicled the creation of Terry Gilliam's "12 Monkeys." in a documentary called "The Hamster Factor and Other Tales of Twelve Monkeys."

"Entertaining and illuminating"—**Time Out: The Hamster Factor and Other Tales of Twelve Monkeys[189]**

Critical Reviews of The Zero Theorem

Jason Bailey, Flavorwire: "While it doesn't match his previous masterpieces, it frequently manages to recapture the anti-authoritarian spirit and whirling dervish quality of his best work."[190]

185   *https://www.timeout.com/film/reviews/79888/12_monkeys.html*

186   *https://www.thetimes.co.uk/article/film-review-12-monkeys-1995-gzzx7rhkl*

187   *https://www.nytimes.com/1995/12/27/movies/film-review-a-time-traveler-with-bad-news.html*

188   *Gilliam on Gilliam Christie, Gilliam, pp.226–230*

189   *https://www.timeout.com/movies/the-hamster-factor-and-other-tales-of-twelve-monkeys*

190   *https://www.flavorwire.com/477879/the-zero-theorem-is-terry-gilliam-at-his-gilliam-est*

Ty Burr, *Boston Globe*: "Say this for Terry Gilliam: Even when he repeats himself, he's unique."[191]

Wesley Morris, Grantland: "The culture's caught up to Gilliam. Everybody's doing Orwell now. But Gilliam's appropriation feels both aptly skeptical and unfashionably utopian."[192]

Brandy McDonnell, *The Oklahoman*: "Although dystopian futures have hit the film franchise fast track these days, director Terry Gilliam has been portending a miserable, unjust future since 1985 – and with biting humor and a bizarrely colorful style."[193]

"What's happened is the industry has become very much like society - there are the rich [films] and the cheap ones and the middle-budget films have been squeezed out of existence." **—Terry Gilliam**[194]

In an interview with Alex Suskind for Indiewire in 2014, Terry Gilliam said, "Well, it's funny, this trilogy was never something I ever said, but it's been repeated so often it's clearly true [laughs]. I don't know who started it but once it started it never stopped."[195]

"Lost in La Mancha" is a 2002 documentary that chronicles Terry Gilliam's initial attempt to create a film adaptation of Miguel de Cervantes' renowned novel "Don Quixote," titled "The Man Who Killed Don Quixote." Originally intended as a behind-the-scenes look at the making of Gilliam's film during its pre-production and filming stages, the documentary sadly had to be retitled "Lost in La

---

[191]   *https://www.bostonglobe.com/arts/movies/2014/10/09/movie-review-gilliam-re-hash-the-zero-theorem-still-adds-something/*

[192]   *https://grantland.com/hollywood-prospectus/movie-review-maze-runner-zero-theorem-drop-skeleton-twins/*

[193]   *Brandy McDonnell https://eu.oklahoman.com/*

[194]   *Jeremy Kay, "Terry Gilliam, The Zero Theorem"(18 May 2013). https://www.screendaily.com/features/terry-gilliam-the-zero-theorem/5056232.article*

[195]   *Alex Suskind (September 17, 2014). "Interview: Terry Gilliam On The Zero Theorem, Avoiding Facebook, Don Quixote And His Upcoming Autobiography." IndieWire.*

Mancha" as Gilliam was unable to complete the project. The film was ultimately released as an independent piece.

Keith Fulton and Louis Pepe served as the directors and writers of "Lost in La Mancha," utilizing the parallels between Gilliam's struggle to create "Don Quixote" and the character's own quest to become a hero. The documentary features appearances by Johnny Depp, Jean Rochefort, and Vanessa Paradis, all of whom were originally cast in The "Man Who Killed Don Quixote." Jeff Bridges lent his voice as the narrator.

Despite the setbacks chronicled in "Lost in La Mancha," Gilliam finally succeeded in making "The Man Who Killed Don Quixote," which was released in 2018. Fulton and Pepe created a follow-up documentary called "He Dreams of Giants," which covers Gilliam's entire journey in developing the Quixote project.

"This is more a film about an internal struggle in an artist's mind. What is it like for an artist to be standing on the brink of actually finishing this project finally? [...] Even on the set we would say the conflicts raging around Terry right now of making the movie are not nearly as interesting as what's going on inside his head."[196]—**Louis Pepe**

---

[196] *"'Lost in La Mancha' Sequel to Capture Terry Gilliam's Most Recent Struggles Making 'The Man Who Killed Don Quixote'." (11 May 2018).*

Discovering the Complexities of Time, Madness, and Identity: A Study of Twelve Monkeys

The movie "Twelve Monkeys" guided by Terry Gilliam and written by David and Janet Peoples is a captivating expedition of time identity and the fragile nature of presence. This dystopian work of art was originally released in 1995. It features impressive performances from Bruce Willis, Madeline Stowe, and Brad Pitt. Their portrayals bring depth and complexity to the characters they personify. In this essay we will delve into the nature of Willis', Stowe's and Pitt's characters as well as Gilliams's visionary instructions and the thought-provoking movie script penned by David and Janet Peoples.

At the heart of "Twelve Monkeys" Bruce Willis takes on the role of James Cole, a convict sent back in time from an apocalyptic future to prevent a deadly virus from obliterating humanity. With his nuanced performance Willis catches Cole's despair, confusion, and vulnerability with amazing accuracy. As Cole grapples with the complexities of time followed with the complexities bordering his objective Willis instills his character with raw intensity and psychological depth that leaves an indelible impression on audiences.

Madeline Stowe delivers efficiency, as Dr. Kathryn Railly, a psychiatrist who finds herself knotted in Cole's objective. Stowe brings a feeling of heat and understanding to her personality, supplying a visibility amidst the chaotic journey of Cole. As Railly attempts to understand the occasions unfolding around her Stowe represents interest and resolution showcasing her personality's transformation from sceptic to follower. Through her nuanced performance Stowe adds depth to the film's expedition of destiny and specific choice encouraging viewers to doubt the nature of reality and the impact of film.

In a role that defines his profession Brad Pitt delivers a fascinating efficiency as Jeffrey Goines, an eccentric person with a psychological problem who aligns himself with Cole. Pitt's portrayal is a display of regulated turmoil effortlessly transitioning between moments of unbalanced power and reflective calmness. With his animated motions, speech shipment and puncturing gaze, Pitt commands interest in every scene producing an unpredictable and enigmatic presence that mesmerizes target markets throughout the film.

The lustre of "Twelve Monkeys" lies not only in the remarkable efficiencies yet also in Terry Gilliam's visionary direction and the idea-prompting screenplay, by David and Janet Peoples.

Gilliam's distinct aesthetic style appears in his movies with its imagery, complex collection styles and innovative electronic camera angles. It immerses the audience in a haunting world that obscures the boundaries between reality and impression. The focus to information and capability to develop a timeless atmosphere includes depth and splendor to the tale. Additionally, the movie script masterfully weaves together motifs of insanity, memory and morality leading to an extraordinary story.

"Twelve Monkeys" surpasses category conventions to end up being a true cinematic masterpiece. The exceptional performances by Bruce Willis, Madeline Stowe and Brad Pitt combined with Terry Gilliam's instructions and the thought-stimulating movie script by David and Janet Peoples delve into extensive questions regarding time, identification and what it means to be human. As a sustaining work of art "Twelve Monkeys" continues to mesmerize with its vision and provocative styles. It has rightfully made its place as a classic, in movie history.

Peoples' Madness: An Interview with Janet and David Peoples on Twelve Monkeys

Janet and David Peoples are screenwriters known for their meticulous attention to detail and ability to create rich characters and explore themes of morality, redemption, and the human condition. They dive into the complexities of human nature and challenge conventional notions of right and wrong. Their contributions to cinema have had a lasting impact, earning them recognition and admiration from both audiences and fellow filmmakers. Their screenplays are celebrated for their depth, intelligence, and emotional resonance, cementing their place together as two of the most respected writers in the industry.

Q: Twelve Monkey Memories:

David Peoples: I had worked previously with a very good producer, whom we admired a lot named Chuck Roven. And Chuck had partnered with a guy named Bob Kosberg on a project, and this project was La Jetée. Bob had been emailing and having a dialogue with Chris Marker, and they wanted us to look at La Jetée. Anyway, Chris knew nothing about us. Kosberg had had a dialogue with him. Kosberg and Chuck Roven sent us a videotape of La Jetée; we had missed it in the 60s because we were raising two kids. And we missed a lot of movies. And that was a famous one that we knew about, but we'd never seen it. We got this bad video of La Jetée. And we watched it. And it was, in its own way, a masterpiece. We thought it was terrific. We thought there was no Hollywood movie in it. If there had ever been a Hollywood movie in it, James Cameron had already done it with Terminator. In fact, we even wondered if he'd taken Terminator from La Jetée, so we said no. And Chuck Roven is a very persuasive guy and someone we respect enormously. He asked us to reconsider our "no." And so we did what we do: we said, "Okay, we'll give it another shot to see if there's anything we can think of to make a movie out of this": a Hollywood movie out of it. And what we do is take a weekend, and we pretend somebody's kidnapped our kids. And that if we don't come up with a story by Monday, we're not going to get our kids back, right. That's just a discipline we use to try and make ourselves work hard and see if we can do it. And we assumed we couldn't.

But then in the course of the weekend, we knew we didn't want to make some post-Holocaust thing. It had been done so many times. It wasn't that it was bad. It was great, and in Terminator, and Terminator 2 and all that stuff. But it had been done so much. It was just not interesting. It seemed like an old trope. And then it came to us: the vision of a city with wild animals roaming around—just as an image and everything—we got excited about the idea of germs doing that to the humans, and the humans hiding underground. And so we had the beginning of a story. And Jan will tell you that in Berkeley you will walk around, and you meet people who have strange points of view. And Jan, you want to talk about that.

Janet Peoples: There are several things. We lived right around the corner from a university. And one, they were doing animal experiments, and there was an animal lab and people were protesting that and everything. David and I also as a background thing had been interested in the Spanish flu and what had happened. And what would happen if it happened again. As far as walking around Berkeley, this is before the days of all the homeless camps, encampments, and everything. But in Berkeley, there were always people who were out of their minds, as it were, perhaps, on the corner with leaflets, or just proselytizing, and saying the end of the world is coming, right, so we were very influenced by these characters.

David Peoples: We began to imagine the person who comes up to you and tells you that he comes from the future, and that the human race is going to be wiped out in a few weeks by this germ. That person believes what he's saying is true. And so we thought, well, how interesting to look at this story from his point of view. Either he thinks he was—or he was—in some sort of future situation. And now he's back here warning us. And that was a very interesting point of view to see. And then we thought about our psychiatrist, and we thought of the wonderful drama of this guy who thinks he comes from the future, and the psychiatrist who thinks he's crazy. And then them switching their points of view so that he's persuaded her he comes from the future. And she's persuaded him that he's just crazy. And we enjoyed that whole concept.

And out of that we told Chuck Roven and Bob Kosberg: Well, we'll try it, we'll do it. Then we got the shock of our life. Because normally, when this happens, when they invite a writer, they invited us to come down to LA, right, and meet and so on. And they said Chris Marker would be there and everything. But normally, no producer would ever bring the writers down if he didn't have the rights to the material. And so, we assumed that they had made a deal with Chris and that he wanted some Hollywood writers to write this Hollywood movie. We got down to the Chateau Marmont, and we met Chris Marker who was an absolute charming man and very regal and important, and we were huge admirers of his film. He was at the Chateau Marmont, also. But it turned out he had nothing but contempt for Hollywood. Except for one movie, which was Vertigo. He thought that was a good movie. Anything else was just junk. So, Jan and I left Chris's suite in a bit of confusion. What the hell are we doing here? What's this about? We're writers and the producers are supposed to have the rights to this. And they're trusting us to somehow talk him into giving them the rights, which they never told us. So, we go down to the lobby of the chateau.

Janet Peoples: And we run into this guy named Tom Luddy, who is the head of Telluride Film Festival, and who also lived in Berkeley.

David Peoples: He was an international figure and knew all the directors.

Janet Peoples: So, it's like, we run into Tom, just as David and I are saying, well, what are we supposed to do? Are we supposed to check out and go back to Berkley? We run into Tom Luddy, a neighbour and a friend, and he knew Chris. Chris was a good friend of his. We told him a little bit about why we were down there and everything and Chris had no intention of having a Hollywood movie made from La Jetée. Tom Luddy listened very seriously and everything and was like, well, I tell you what, Chris is a friend, and Chris loves Francis Coppola. And Francis is in town. Let's have dinner tonight. So, we thought, Oh, okay. And we went back to our room and just sat there, still puzzled over what we were supposed to do, right? And we get a phone call from Tom Luddy. And he said, meet us at six-thirty or seven at Joss, which was a restaurant that we loved in Hollywood. And so, at that time, we go down to the restaurant, and we walk in. And there's a very large table where a bunch of writers and directors are assembling. Nobody knows why they're there. Just a nice dinner. There's Francis Coppola at the head of the table. He's talking menus, food, and wine with the chefs; this is very important.

We sit down and we're all just chatting. Chris Marker comes in with Tom Luddy. Chris sits at one end of the table. And Francis is at the other end of the table. And we're just all sitting there, and the wine comes in. Everyone's drinking and now the food comes in; the food is just exquisite. Absolutely wonderful. Everyone's having a good time. And then Francis suddenly says to Chris: Janet, and David are here, and they want to make a film based on La Jetée. They are good people, so you should let them to do it.

And there were no producers there. There were no producers at that table, except for Tom Luddy. And that then afterwards, everything just proceeded, and I'll have to tell you the story of what we heard, but we can't confirm. We think this is the only contract that's ever been made at Universal Studios that was made with a signed napkin. No lawyers. The only thing that Chris hated more than lawyers was psychiatrists.

David Peoples: Francis Coppola should get a lot of credit for Twelve Monkeys, and so should Tom Luddy. Anyway, they got Chris on board, in principle, but then he had to work this out. And as Jan says, he was not going to deal with a bunch of lawyers. And Chuck got him to sign a napkin, and Chuck to his credit, managed somehow to get Universal to work it all out and make it happen. And that's how we came aboard La Jetée.

Q: When you first met Terry Gilliam, what was your reaction? Had you seen Brazil and his other movies?

David Peoples: We had seen Time Bandits, which we thought was an absolute work of genius. We loved Time Bandits. And I think we'd seen Brazil also after that. And so, we were at the Chateau Marmont again—the cradle of cinema—and we were in our suite, and Terry Gilliam was staying at the Chateau and wanted to meet me because I had written Unforgiven. And he just wanted to come and say hello to us. So he came by, and we met him. And we were thrilled to meet a great master like him. And in the course of it, he said, "Well, what are you working on now?" And we said, we're working on this nut who thinks he's from the future, and the psychiatrist who gets persuaded he is from the future. And Terry was interested in that, right? And wanted us to send it to him when we finished it.

He was committed to doing his dream project, Tale of Two Cities, for Warner Brothers. And that was what he wanted to do most, as much as he liked our script. So that had passed. And we had always thought there were only a few directors who could do it. And one of our favourites was Tony Scott. And we were trying to get Tony to do it. But Universal was reluctant to deal with Tony, ironically, right? And so, we didn't have a picture and everything until Terry's Tale of Two Cities was cancelled at Warner Brothers. And so Terry came back to us. And in the meantime, we'd done a little rewrite for Chuck and Bob. But Terry looked at it and liked the original. He'd had a bad relationship with Universal because of the Brazil thing. And it was a triumph on Chuck Roven's part that he was able to get Universal to accept Terry as the director.

Janet Peoples: We had a wonderful, wonderful executive that we were dealing with there: Casey Silver. There were a lot of people who liked the script and liked the project and everything. But everyone was unsure that this was going to be a project that anyone could understand the film.

David Peoples: It was very risky. And it was riskier than we understood until once we'd seen it. And we realized just how confusing the script was, and just how clear Terry Gilliam made it. Terry himself is a wonderful writer. He didn't do rewriting or anything. He gave us suggestions, and we made some changes. But the bottom line is he knows how to tell a story—like few directors do—and most of the directors who are visionaries, and obviously Jim Cameron would be the exception and so would be Christopher Nolan. They both are visionaries, but they also know how to tell a story. Terry is a master and he pulled it off and in hindsight it's unbelievable how well he did it, and that there's nobody else who could have done it that well. Nobody.

Janet Peoples: During the making of the script, the writing of the script and showing things to Chris, we became friends with Chris Marker, and he even came to Berkeley several times and visited us. In La Jetée the woman is just beautiful. She has no job. She's a male dream. But in a Hollywood movie, you got to have somebody who is flesh and blood. And so, we turned her into a psychiatrist, because that fit our notion of the movie and how it could work.

David Peoples: Chris Marker was most supportive of us. In spite of the fact he obviously had great trepidations. And I think he was surprised that he came to like the movie, but he did.

Janet Peoples: He loved Madeline Stowe in the movie. She made the movie. People talk about the male stars and everything. But her character was very difficult.

David Peoples: She is not the obvious great actor in the movie, but she certainly carries it as much as Bruce or Brad, who get most of the credit. And not that they weren't brilliant. They were brilliant. But Madeline Stowe was the glue that kept that movie going. Her believability, and her commitment to that role and who she was, is just breathtaking.

Q: Memories of Bruce Willis:

David Peoples: I'll tell you the truth. Nobody would have done that any better than Bruce. He's an amazing actor. Although Bruce usually got $20,000,000 for starring in big Hollywood action movies, he did Twelve Monkeys for a much smaller amount because he really wanted to do it. He is a great actor. Bruce Willis plays a more subtle and controlled role in the movie In Country. It's a departure from some of his more action-oriented roles, and it really showcases his range as an actor. A wonderful actor and he was at the top of his game in Twelve Monkeys.

Janet Peoples: We had table reads. This is in the rehearsals prior to the shooting. And we would go around and around and round, and everyone was on board with who they were and everything. And Bruce was being like, I just don't get it. Why would I? Why would I do this? Why would I do that and everything, and all of a sudden we realized that when we were writing the script, we wanted things in that made it clear how he had been a certain age when he went underground. And it was very difficult for us to do and everything. I said, "Bruce, listen to this: How old were you when you went underground? That's what you knew. You knew the music of that day. You knew the candy of that day. You knew all the games that the kids played at that day. You didn't know anything after that, other than being underground." He said, "I got it. I'm nine years old." I said, "You're a grown man. But you were. That's what you were when you went underground." He said, "I got it." And it's like—and then I tried to talk: "No, no, no. I got it. I got it." And he did. He was great.

David Peoples: The Hamster Factor was a wonderful documentary. And what I think I liked most about it was, most of the making of movies don't show you post-production. But this showed just how tough Terry was. And even when we were scared and thought he shouldn't change the movie, he didn't: he just stuck by his guns. He's as tough as nails: that came out in that process.

David Peoples: Terry Gilliam, that's a great filmmaker. Now. One of the reasons that film was a success is because the two women at Universal who were in charge of marketing were brilliant. And they knew to be very careful to not set it up as a Bruce Willis action-adventure movie, because they knew that an audience would come in, hate it, be disappointed and it would get bad word of mouth and then we're just down the toilet. They set it up to sell it not as a Bruce Willis adventure movie, but as a Terry Gilliam movie. And as that it was terrific. It was not successful like these huge, Star Wars kind of stuff or anything, but it was very successful. They carefully sculpted an audience for it that was going there to see a Terry Gilliam movie and they got a Terry Gilliam movie with Bruce Willis in it. So they did a beautiful job.

Janet Peoples: The business of getting your audience and everything is absolutely incredible. Because recently—and this is an aside, not about Twelve Monkeys, but it's getting a right audience—happened in this country to get people back to the movie theatres with Oppenheimer and Barbie. Who would have thought, right? Well, they got the right audiences. People wanted to go see a Chris Nolan film and afterward the executives said, "Who the hell would think that anyone would want to go out and watch a movie about a bunch of scientists making an atom bomb in real life?" Right? And it's sort of like, well, they got the right audience in there. They got all the young women to go back into the movie theatres because they had stayed out during the pandemic.

Q: I remember as well, that also with the cast, you had Christopher Plummer. And you had David Morse; you had quite a cast outside of the main stars as well?

David Peoples: That's Terry; he knows what he's doing. And what was our reaction to the performance in the film? Well, Brad was brilliant, and did some really good ad libs in the mental institution that blew our minds; we wish we'd written them where he rattles the games. His adlib was brilliant in that scene. Obviously. And we've already said that Bruce was terrific. But Madeline Stowe just stepped up and she doesn't get the attention she deserves.

Q: I think the character of Jeffrey Goines, that character was inspired from another script if I'm right?

Janet Peoples: I had written a script in which there is this young, idealistic eco kid who wants to save the world and save the forests, and everything: doesn't know what he's doing, goes off on his own. He likes some redwood trees in a forest, it's going to be cut down. And one of the tree cutters comes in; his saw hits a nail, and the tree cutter dies, hits the spike, and falls and dies. And it's the story of this young kid. I wrote a serious movie although the guy was wacko. David said, you know who this is? And he said, it's your wacko nut, eco nut and everything. And so that's how Goines made it into the script.

David Peoples: Goines is a name you'll see in all our films, because David Lance Goines was a good friend. He just passed away recently, but we loved his name. And it's not ethnic, but it's memorable. It's not like Smith or Johnson. And Goines just seemed a wonderful name. You'll see him in Hero. He's a judge in Hero. He loved his part in Twelve Monkeys—that Jeffrey Goines role. And when he died, some of his people said, "Put a big poster up," because he was a poster artist and very famous, and they put up a poster that says *Fucking Goines, what's he done now?* Which I guess is a quote from the movie, but it was there on his door beautifully done: *Fucking Goines, what's he done now?* and he's passed away and so on. It was a remarkable experience, but he loved himself in that role. And he appears in so many of our scripts, the name Goines. Our son-in-law has a unique name. There's no other person with that name in the United States. So we use his name from time to time, but it's a difficult name. Anyway. We're moving on.

Q: On the Twelve Monkeys TV series:

Janet Peoples: By the way we were approached if we wanted to do a series, and we said we didn't. Then we did read the pilot script. And we were asked what we thought of it, we said, "Well, it's a different thing than what we do. It's different than the movie."

David Peoples: We looked at it in the first place. When we first were asked about it, we didn't think it was a good idea. And nobody ever offered us a going project to do but at any rate, they did have it written. And I think we read the draft once and as far as we were concerned, it wasn't Twelve Monkeys. When we watched the pilot, we thought it was very interesting. And we did think it used our characters, which annoyed us that we weren't getting paid for using our characters. It wasn't anything like what Twelve Monkeys was. Twelve Monkeys was about a guy who might have been deranged, right? Who might have been from the future. Or maybe he wasn't right. No, maybe he was crazy. And I remember, at any rate, the series we saw was pure sci-fi: based on magical things, shooting people back and forth in space. Whereas in ours, it was ambiguous, suggesting that the Book of Revelations had been written by people coming from the future, but where they were supposed to be going, so we were having fun with that. And that was all missing from the television show as far as we could see.

Janet Peoples: We never watched anything other than the first pilot. And people never contacted us or said how wonderful it was and were we involved.

David Peoples: Anyway, the Twelve Monkey series was, in our view, pretty divorced. It was a good series. I think people liked it. And so clearly, it was a success on its own terms. But it wasn't anything like the premise of Twelve Monkeys, which was quite different.

I love the music and the production design. The design for Twelve Monkeys obviously had a bit of a Brazil vibe. One of Terry Gilliam's previous films.

Janet Peoples: Gilliam did the design with the design people. I mean, that's his look. We also put music in the script.

David Peoples: Terry replaced one of the songs with the Louis Armstrong song It's a Beautiful World, which I think he was right to do. It was better. We did have Blueberry Hill in there in the script. The beautiful opening and the theme of the Twelve Monkeys. I mean, that has nothing to do with us. That's Terry Gilliam at his maddest and most wonderful with his composer. Terry Gilliam: we can't speak highly enough of him.

Q: Did you ever want to go into directing, Janet?

Janet Peoples: I really didn't think about it. At one point there was somebody that came to me, and they were doing something, but I actually can't remember anything more than *did I want to do this?* And then we talked about it. And then afterwards, I didn't pay any attention to it. But I do know now that the directors that we like are able to see things artistically—if that makes sense to you—that they have some vision that they can see and they can take something that they see on the paper visually, and can enlarge in their heads. The business of that chair that Terry had in Twelve Monkeys for Bruce to sit in that went up and down with the scientists in that room and everything—I was blown away by it. It's like not how I had imagined it. But if you said, but how did you imagine it? I didn't.

David Peoples: That Christmas and the angel and rising up in the department store, that was magic. That was entirely Terry's work in Twelve Monkeys. And we were just shocked and amazed; and we loved it. But going back to Janet and directing. Certainly, I understand what she's saying. And what she's saying is true. But it's also true that Janet has the kind of mind that can manage people, and I don't, so she would have been a better director than me in many ways.

Janet Peoples: I think I would have been a better producer.

David Peoples: But at any rate, all I'm saying is I certainly wasn't a director. Although I don't think I did a bad job. I just didn't do a terrific job.

Q: Discuss your memories of working in the hospital and kind of how it influenced your work on the screenplay for Twelve Monkeys.

David Janet: Well, one of the things that we both experienced, that we directly put into the screenplay was: There would be a meeting—a round table meeting—at the hospital with a bunch of doctors sitting around, and they would bring in a new patient, and they would ask questions of the new patient to determine the patient's condition. And I remember that they were sitting around the table. And before the patient came in one said to the other one, "You know what day it is? And the other one, "Yes, Friday. What date? Oh, the seventh, great, okay," and so on. And then the guy would come in, the patient would come in. And they would ask, among other things, what day it was, and if he was confused and he didn't know the day that would be a mark against them. And yet the doctor himself had to ask his colleagues what day it was. Sorry, I'm not saying this so well, but one of the experiences about being in the mental institution is except by what people were wearing, you couldn't always tell who an inmate was and who was a doctor or an orderly or something. It wasn't a clear line of who was crazy and who wasn't.

Janet Peoples: I think that the mental institution that we worked at was a state hospital, and it didn't have very much money. And most of the patients that were there on the acute ward—not the chronic ward, but the acute ward—were tranquilized. And they just were completely out of it because they were tranquilized. When the medicines would wear off, or the medicines didn't take effect, they were out of their minds. They had hallucinations and everything. And as David said, the staff and the doctors who would come in very often seemed as nutty as the patient. The doctors would come and be like, "Where did I leave my nice, my suitcase? That's no—I meant my briefcase: where did I leave my briefcase?" I'm just saying that was just normal behaviour. If it hadn't been in a mental institution, we wouldn't say anything of it. But because we were working on this particular ward, or in this particular building, their actions very often mirror the patient. We were very, very young at the time. And I wasn't working there. I was doing an internship there. I was not working there. I mean, you know, I wasn't getting paid for working there. I just was there for a three-month period, learning things.

David Peoples: She was doing her mental institution training later on, after we got married. After we met in the hospital. I worked in that same mental institution. But I was working there, I was getting paid, but I was completely untrained. And I didn't know what the hell I was doing. Anyway, it was an experience. For us, the experience was it wasn't as crazy as we expected it to be. It was not as different as outside as it was inside, but you were close with the people. And they were sometimes very troubled, but they weren't always acting crazy. They weren't acting that much crazier than our family stood on the outside a little. [laughter]

Janet Peoples: There was one patient that I had; every day he would say the same thing. And the first time that he approached me and told me this fabulous story I was taken in by it. It was quite wonderful. But the second day when he approached me as if I was a complete stranger, and he told me the exact same story, word for word. And then the third day I was saying to him, I think I've heard this story before, and he got very upset. He said, I've never met you before in my whole life. Now, other than that, he seemed like a very reasonable person the first time I met him, but when we started writing Twelve Monkeys, I remembered that and when we were doing the character of the guy who was telling the story to Brad Pitt, I had remembered that patient with a great deal of fondness.

Q: I remember the character that sort of cuddles up to Bruce Willis in the film. And I remember he says he's from some planet, and I remember that. So that person had inspired you, obviously, one of the influences of Twelve Monkeys.

Janet Peoples: The patient that I'm referring to didn't say he was from another planet, but he did have a few little kinks in his story, that were not actually true, that you knew this could happen. He was disturbed to be sure, but not as disturbed as I came to understand he was later on.

David Peoples: [Laughter] My family would remind me of the people in the institution when I got home after work. And they would have little funny things they would say. And I just had this feeling that they were just like people in the mental institution. And yet, they haven't had the incident that got those people in. If you were to have a terrible incident, and you acted out and you threw all your clothes out of the window in your house, or you stood in the middle of the street, in an angry rage in those days, you could have been committed to a mental institution, when in fact, that was a single incident in your life, and not something you did regularly. But now you're in a mental institution, and you're just a guy who had a bad day. Well, I mean, it's not as simple as that. But that's what it felt like in those days. It couldn't have happened now. It's a very different world.

Janet Peoples: Most of the patients there had psychotic breaks, and they were schizophrenic, and they were just being treated with Thorazine. That was an earlier time of treating drugs, using drugs, and they mostly were just trained; there was no other—or sometimes electroshock therapy—but they weren't really diagnosed into individually or correctly, and they probably didn't have much of a chance of getting better. It would be completely different today.

David Peoples: I distinctly remember being extremely impressed with Billy Bob Thornton's short film. Not the movie he eventually made, but a short called Some Folks Call It a Sling Blade. In that short, the late great actor J.T. Walsh delivered an exceptional performance as a mentally ill individual. It truly is a masterpiece and featured Molly Ringwald, who had previously appeared in the film Pretty in Pink. It's quite remarkable, and I personally believe it surpasses the subsequent feature film.

The Blood of Heroes/Salute of the Jugger

Film Credits

Director & Writer

David Webb Peoples

Producer

Charles Roven

Executive Producer

Brian Rosen

Composer

Todd Boekelheide

Cinematographer

David Eggby

Editor

Richard Francis-Bruce

Production Designer

John Stoddart

Costume Designer

Terry Ryan

Makeup Department

Robyn Austin	...	makeup artist
Nik Dorning	...	makeup artist
Marjory Hamlin	...	makeup artist
Brita Kingsbury	...	hair: second unit
Kerrie MacFarlane	...	makeup assistant
Bob McCarron	...	special makeup designer
Debbie Nathan	...	makeup assistant
Wendy Sainsbury	...	makeup artist
Yvonne Savage	...	hairdresser
Sonja Smuk	...	makeup artist
Lesley Vanderwalt	...	makeup artist
Michael Westmore	...	special makeup effects designer
Paul Williams	...	hairdresser
Michael Burnett	...	special makeup effects assistant (uncredited)

Production Management

Tic Carroll	...	unit manager
Marty Hornstein (as Martin Hornstein)	...	executive in charge of production
Carol Hughes	...	unit production manager
Kelley Smith-Wait	...	post production supervisor (as Kelley M. Smith)

Second Unit Director or Assistant Director

Keith Heygate	...	first assistant director
Gregor Jordan	...	fourth assistant director (as Greg Jordan)
Guy Norris	...	second unit director
Maria Phillips	...	third assistant director
Adrian Pickersgill	...	first assistant director: second unit (as Adrien Pickergill)
P.J. Voeten	...	second assistant director

Art Department

Michael Ashton	...	carpenter
Michael John Burgess	...	prop maker
Warren Field	...	concept model maker
Justin Fitzpatrick	...	art department assistant
Alan Fleming	...	construction manager
Colin Gibson	...	standby props
Donni Gonzales	...	assistant standby props
Adam Grace	...	model maker
Pauline Grebert	...	prop maker
Paul Jones	...	art department assistant
Fiona Kemp	...	scenic artist
Steve Lyons	...	storyboard artist
Helen Macaskill	...	props buyer
Gerald Marr	...	carpenter
Bob McCarron	...	props design: special animal

Frances McDonald	...	art department coordinator
Jock McLachlan	...	props buyer / props dresser
Warwick Miller	...	carpenter
Julieanne Mills	...	model maker assistant
Gillian Nicholas	...	prop maker
Brian Nickless	...	assistant art director
Michael O'Kane	...	scenic artist
Bob Paton	...	construction foreman
Luigi Pittorino	...	draughtsperson (as Luigi Pittorina)
Robert Podhadsky	...	carpenter (as Robert Podhajsky)
David Rutherford	...	model maker
David Scott	...	carpenter
David Stenning	...	carpenter
Michael Tolerton	...	props buyer
David Tremont	...	model maker
Bill Undery	...	scenic artist
John D. Williams	...	props assistant
Michael Wood	...	brushhand
Norman Wray	...	standby carpenter

Sound Department

Mark Berger	...	supervising re-recording mixer
Jay Boekelheide	...	sound designer / supervising sound editor
Lloyd Carrick	...	production sound mixer
Kim Cascone	...	additional apprentice sound editor

Scott Chandler	...	foley engineer
Cherilene Chen	...	additional apprentice sound editor
Luis Colina	...	foley editor
Clare C. Freeman	...	assistant dialogue editor (as Clare Freeman)
Kristen Gerstner	...	additional apprentice sound editor
Chris Goldsmith	...	boom operator
Danny Kopelson	...	re-recording mixer
Barbara McBane	...	dialogue editor
Devon Miller	...	first assistant sound editor
Marnie Moore	...	foley artist
Douglas Murray	...	sound effects editor
David Parker	...	re-recording mixer
John Roesch	...	foley artist
Michael Rosen	...	foley engineer
Paige Sartorius	...	dialogue editor
Michael Semanick	...	foley engineer
Dennie Thorpe	...	foley artist
Pam Uzzell	...	additional apprentice sound editor
Matthew White	...	apprentice sound editor
Philip Rogers	...	sound recordist (uncredited)

Special Effects

Neville Maxwell	...	special effects coordinator

Stunts

Danny Baldwin	...	stunts
Peter Chen	...	stunts
Mitch Deans	...	stunts
Ollie Hall	...	stunts
Jeff Jensen	...	stunts
Rocky McDonald	...	stunts
Guy Norris	...	stunt coordinator
Richard Norton	...	stunts
Chris Peters	...	stunts
Steve Rackman	...	stunts
Lee Rice	...	stunts
Glenn Ruehland	...	co-stunt coordinator
Josef Schwaiger	...	stunts
Greg Stuart	...	stunts
Don Vaughn	...	stunts
Mark Warren	...	stunts
James Webb	...	stunts
Sue Baldwin	...	stunts (uncredited)
Tony Yuen	...	stunts (uncredited)

Camera and Electrical Department

John Breslin	...	clapper/loader: main unit
Gary Carden	...	first assistant grip
Katrina Crook	...	clapper/loader: second unit

Phil Cross	...	camera operator (as Philip M. Cross) / steadicam operator (as Philip M. Cross)
Ian Dewhurst	...	gaffer
Derry Field	...	focus puller: main unit
Martin Forster	...	third assistant grip
Paul Gantner	...	assistant electrician (as Paul J. Gantner)
Frank Hammond	...	director of photography: second unit
Guy Hancock	...	assistant electrician
Grahame Litchfield	...	key grip
Lex Martin	...	best boy
Nick Mayo	...	focus puller: camera b (as Nicholas Mayo)
Robert McFarlane	...	still photographer
Nick Payne	...	third electrician
Mark Ramsey	...	second assistant grip
Adrien Seffrin	...	clapper/loader: camera b (as Adrien Quinn Seffrin)
Lewis Sparkes	...	assistant electrician
Peter Terakes	...	camera assistant: second unit
Peter Stott	...	camera maintenance (uncredited)

Casting Department

Alison Barrett	...	casting: Australia
Nikki Barrett	...	casting assistant (as Nicky Barrett)
Jeff Block	...	casting assistant
Judith Cruden	...	extras casting

Suzanne Ryan	...	casting assistant
Bonnie Timmermann	...	casting: USA

Costume and Wardrobe Department

Peter Bevan	...	wardrobe buyer
Tom Collins	...	wardrobe assistant
Kate Green	...	machinist: #1
Kathy James	...	wardrobe supervisor
Helen Mather	...	machinist: #2
Devina Maxwell	...	wardrobe assistant
Kerri Mazzocco	...	stand-by wardrobe (as Kerri Barnett)
Lisa Meagher	...	wardrobe assistant
Liz Neate	...	machinist: #3
Shane Phillips	...	wardrobe assistant
Andrew Short	...	stand-by wardrobe
Peter Thonasson	...	wardrobe assistant
Steven Vella	...	wardrobe assistant
Ross Wallace	...	wardrobe assistant

Editorial Department

Donah Bassett	...	negative cutter
Luis Colina	...	second assistant editor: U.S.
Patricia A. Galvin	...	first assistant editor: U.S. (as Patricia Galvin)
David Grusovin	...	second assistant editor: Australia
Louise Innes	...	first assistant editor: Australia
Richard Ritchie	...	color timer (as Dick Ritchie)

Location Management

| Robin Clifton | ... | location manager |

Music Department

Mark Adler	...	conductor: orchestral ensembles / orchestrations
Todd Boekelheide	...	music recorded by / orchestrations
Danny Kopelson	...	music recorded by
Larry London	...	musician liaison
David Luke	...	music recorded by

Script and Continuity Department

| Melanie Brown | ... | continuity: second unit |
| Jo Weeks | ... | continuity |

Additional Crew

Penny Attfield	...	production secretary
Penny Carl	...	production accountant
Mandy Carter	...	accounts assistant
Evanne Chesson	...	animal handler
Andy Clarke	...	safety officer
Anna Deakins	...	production assistant
Gabrielle Dunn	...	production liaison: Sydney
Lee Elliott	...	masseuse
John Faithfull	...	caterer: Sydney (as Johnny Faithfull)

Kathleen Herd	...	production liaison: Los Angeles (as Kathleen C. Heard)
David Hutchinson	...	masseuse
Maggie Lake	...	production coordinator
Steve Marcus	...	caterer: Coober Pedy
Maggie McKay	...	nurse (as Maggie MacKay)
Gill McKinlay	...	production accountant
Annie O'Halloran	...	nurse: second unit
Annette Piggot	...	accounts assistant (as Annette Piggott)
Kate Roach	...	caterer: second unit
Alison Robb	...	unit assistant
Ken Robb	...	unit assistant
Arch Roberts	...	safety officer
Salvador Rover	...	assistant: Mr. Roven
Kelley Smith-Wait	...	production coordinator: L.A. (as Kelley M. Smith)
Dougal Thompson	...	unit assistant
Neal Thompson	...	main title designed by
Reel Wheels	...	unit assistant
Valerie Williams	...	supervising accountant
Annie Wright	...	unit publicist
Paulie Zink	...	personal trainer: Joan Chen
Mason Curtis	...	assistant unit manager (uncredited)
Peter Stott	...	projectionist (uncredited)

Below is a list of apocalyptic genre films through the decades:

- *The End of the World (1916)*
- *End of the World (1931)*
- *Deluge (1933)*
- *Things to Come (1936)*
- *Five (1951)*
- *When Worlds Collide (1951)*
- *Captive Women (1952)*
- *Robot Monster (1953)*
- *Day the World Ended (1955)*
- *World Without End (1956)*
- *The Lost Missile (1958)*
- *Teenage Caveman (1958)*
- *On the Beach (1959)*
- *The World, the Flesh and the Devil (1959)*
- *Beyond the Time Barrier (1960)*
- *Last Woman on Earth (1960)*
- *Battle of the Worlds (1961)*
- *The Last War (1961)*
- *The Day the Earth Caught Fire (1961)*
- *The Creation of the Humanoids (1962)*
- *Panic in Year Zero! (1962)*
- *The Day of the Triffids (1962)*
- *This Is Not a Test (1962)*
- *La Jetée (1962)*
- *Ladybug Ladybug (1963)*

- *Dr. Strangelove or: How I Learned To Stop Worrying and Love the Bomb (1964)*
- *The Time Travelers (1964)*
- *Fail-Safe (1964)*
- *The Last Man on Earth (1964)*
- *Crack in the World (1965)*
- *The War Game (1966)*
- *Daleks – Invasion Earth: 2150 A.D. (1966)*
- *In the Year 2889 (1967)*
- *Late August at the Hotel Ozone (1967)*
- *Night of the Living Dead (1968)*
- *Planet of the Apes (1968)*
- *Il seme dell'uomo (1969)*
- *The Bed-Sitting Room (1969)*
- *Colossus: The Forbin Project (1970)*
- *Beneath the Planet of the Apes (1970)*
- *No Blade of Grass (1970)*
- *Gas-s-s-s (1970)*
- *The Andromeda Strain (1971)*
- *Escape from the Planet of the Apes (1971)*
- *The Omega Man (1971)*
- *Glen and Randa (1971)*
- *Beware! The Blob (1972)*
- *A Thief in the Night (1972)*
- *Conquest of the Planet of the Apes (1972)*
- *A Distant Thunder (1972)*
- *Silent Running (1972)*
- *Soylent Green (1973)*

- *Battle for the Planet of the Apes (1973)*
- *Genesis II (1973)*
- *The Final Programme (The Last Days of Man on Earth) (1973)*
- *Zardoz (1974)*
- *Phase IV (1974)*
- *Planet Earth (1974)*
- *Where Have All The People Gone? (1974)*
- *Black Moon (1975)*
- *The Noah (1975)*
- *The Ultimate Warrior (1975)*
- *A Boy and His Dog (1975)*
- *The Late, Great Planet Earth (1976)*
- *Logan's Run (1976)*
- *The People Who Own the Dark (1976)*
- *Damnation Alley (1977)*
- *End of the World (1977)*
- *Holocaust 2000 (1977)*
- *Wizards (1977)*
- *The Last Wave (1977)*
- *Dawn of the Dead (1978)*
- *Invasion of the Body Snatchers (1978)*
- *Mad Max (1979)*
- *Quintet (1979)*
- *Ravagers (1979)*
- *The Shape of Things to Come (1979)*
- *Stalker (1979)*
- *Virus (1980)*
- *Phoenix 2772 (1980)*

- *Image of the Beast (1981)*
- *Escape from New York (1981)*
- *Mad Max 2 (The Road Warrior) (1981)*
- *Malevil (1981)*
- *Battletruck (1982)*
- *World War III (1982)*
- *Café Flesh (1982)*
- *Blade Runner (1982)*
- *1990: The Bronx Warriors (1982)*[1]
- *The Day After (1983)*
- *Le Dernier Combat (1983)*
- *The New Barbarians (1983)*
- *Stryker (1983)*
- *Testament (1983)*
- *The Prodigal Planet (1983)*
- *Exterminators of the Year 3000 (1983)*
- *Das Arche Noah Prinzip (1984)*
- *When the Wind Blows (1984)*
- *Sexmission (1984)*
- *Threads (1984)*
- *Nausicaä of the Valley of the Wind (1984)*
- *Night of the Comet (1984)*
- *The Terminator (1984)*
- *Day of the Dead (1985)*
- *The Quiet Earth (1985)*
- *Mad Max Beyond Thunderdome (1985)*
- *Radioactive Dreams (1985)*
- *Def-Con 4 (1985)*

- *Wheels of Fire (1985)*
- *America 3000 (1986)*
- *Dead Man's Letters (1986)*
- *Fist of the North Star (1986)*
- *Land of Doom (1986)*
- *Solarbabies (1986)*
- *Steel Dawn (1987)*
- *Cherry 2000 (1987)*
- *The Seventh Sign (1988)*
- *Akira (1988)*
- *Miracle Mile (1988)*
- *Hell Comes to Frogtown (1988)*
- *A Visitor to a Museum (1989)*
- *The Blood of Heroes (The Salute of the Jugger) (1989)*
- *Bunker Palace Hôtel (1989)*
- *Cyborg (1989)*
- *Millennium (1989)*
- *Aftershock (1990)*
- *By Dawn's Early Light (1990)*
- *Solar Crisis (1990)*
- *The Handmaid's Tale (1990)*
- *Hardware (1990)*
- *Circuitry Man (1990)*
- *Terminator 2: Judgment Day (1991)*
- *Until the End of the World (1991)*
- *The Rapture (1991)*
- *Neon City (1991)*
- *Delicatessen (1991)*

- *Split Second (1992)*
- *American Cyborg: Steel Warrior (1993)*
- *Body Snatchers (1993)*
- *The Last Border (1993)*
- *Without Warning (1994)*
- *Plughead Rewired: Circuitry Man II (1994)*
- *In the Mouth of Madness (1994)*
- *12 Monkeys (1995)*
- *Sentinel 2099 (1995)*
- *Steel Frontier (1995)*
- *Tank Girl (1995)*
- *Judge Dredd (1995)*
- *Waterworld (1995)*
- *The Prophecy (1995)*
- *The Arrival (1996)*
- *Omega Doom (1996)*
- *Escape from L.A. (1996)*
- *The End of Evangelion (1997)*
- *Invasion (1997)*
- *The Postman (1997)*
- *Future Fear (1997)*
- *Last Night (1998)*
- *The Prophecy 2 (1998)*
- *Six String Samurai (1998)*
- *Beowulf (1999)*
- *Dogma (1999)*
- *End of Days (1999)*
- *The Matrix (1999)*

- *The Omega Code (1999)*
- *Fail Safe (2000)*
- *The Last Warrior (2000)*
- *Left Behind (2000)*
- *Lost Souls (2000)*
- *The Prophecy 3: The Ascent (2000)*
- *On the Beach (2000)*
- *Titan A.E. (2000)*
- *Final Fantasy: The Spirits Within (2001)*
- *Megiddo: The Omega Code 2 (2001)*
- *A.I. Artificial Intelligence (2001)*
- *Blue Gender:The Warrior (2002)*
- *28 Days Later (2002)*
- *The Time Machine (2002)*
- *Reign of Fire (2002)*
- *Resident Evil (2002)*
- *Returner (2002)*
- *Terminator 3: Rise of the Machines (2003)*
- *Dragon Head (2003)*
- *Dreamcatcher (2003)*
- *Save the Green Planet! (2003)*
- *Time of the Wolf (2003)*
- *The Animatrix (2003)*
- *The Matrix Reloaded (2003)*
- *The Matrix Revolutions (2003)*
- *Dawn of the Dead (2004)*
- *The Day After Tomorrow (2004)*
- *Shaun of the Dead (2004)*

- *Resident Evil: Apocalypse (2004)*
- *The Hitchhiker's Guide to the Galaxy (2005)*
- *Æon Flux (2005)*
- *The Prophecy: Forsaken (2005)*
- *War of the Worlds (2005)*
- *Land of the Dead (2005)*
- *Supervolcano (2005)*
- *Children of Men (2006)*
- *Idiocracy (2006)*
- *Right at Your Door (2006)*
- *Solar Attack (2006)*
- *Southland Tales (2006)*
- *Planet Terror (2007)*
- *Tooth and Nail (2007)*
- *The Signal (2007)*
- *The Invasion (2007)*
- *Resident Evil: Extinction (2007)*
- *20 Years After (2007)*
- *The Dark Hour (2007)*
- *28 Weeks Later (2007)*
- *I Am Legend (2007)*
- *Babylon A.D. (2008)*
- *Blindness (2008)*
- *Resident Evil: Degeneration (2008)*
- *WALL-E (2008)*
- *Daybreakers (2008)*
- *Doomsday (2008)*
- *City of Ember (2008)*

- *The Happening (2008)*
- *Pontypool (2008)*
- *The Road (2009)*
- *Pandorum (2009)*
- *Watchmen (2009)*
- *9 (2009)*
- *Knowing (2009)*
- *Zombieland (2009)*
- *2012 (2009)*
- *Terminator Salvation (2009)*
- *Battlestar Galactica: The Plan (2009)*
- *Happy End (2009)*
- *Carriers (2009)*
- *Earth 2100 (2009)*
- *Juan of the Dead (2010)*
- *Monsters (2010)*
- *Stake Land (2010)*
- *Vanishing on 7th Street (2010)*
- *Legion (2010)*
- *Maximum Shame (2010)*
- *The Book of Eli (2010)*
- *Resident Evil: Afterlife (2010)*
- *4:44 Last Day on Earth (2011)*
- *Deadheads (2011)*
- *Perfect Sense (2011)*
- *The Darkest Hour (2011)*
- *The Day (2011)*
- *The Divide (2011)*

- *Melancholia (2011)*
- *Hell (2011)*
- *Take Shelter (2011)*
- *Rise of the Planet of the Apes (2011)*
- *The Cabin in the Woods (2011)*
- *The Hunger Games (2012)*
- *Seeking a Friend for the End of the World (2012)*
- *5 Shells (2012)*
- *Dredd (2012)*
- *It's a Disaster (2012)*
- *Battle: Los Angeles (2012)*
- *Resident Evil: Retribution (2012)*
- *Resident Evil: Damnation (2012)*
- *Cloud Atlas (2012)*
- *Cockneys vs Zombies (2012)*
- *The Battery (2012)*
- *Rapture-Palooza (2013)*
- *The Colony (2013)*
- *These Final Hours (2013)*
- *This Is the End (2013)*
- *After the Dark (2013)*
- *After Earth (2013)*
- *Los Últimos Días (2013)*
- *Antisocial (2013)*
- *Snowpiercer (2013)*
- *Oblivion (2013)*
- *Warm Bodies (2013)*
- *World War Z (2013)*

- *Edge of Tomorrow (2013)*
- *The World's End (2013)*
- *The Host (2013)*
- *Goodbye World (2013)*
- *Die Gstettensaga: The Rise of Echsenfriedl (2014)*
- *Wyrmwood: Road of the Dead (2014)*
- *The Rover (2014)*
- *Zodiac: Signs of the Apocalypse (2014)*
- *X-Men: Days of Future Past (2014)*
- *Young Ones (2014)*
- *Aftermath (2014)*
- *The Maze Runner (2014)*
- *Dawn of the Planet of the Apes (2014)*
- *Interstellar (2014)*
- *The Last Survivors (2014)*
- *Noah (2014)*
- *Autómata (2014)*
- *Scouts Guide to the Zombie Apocalypse (2015)*
- *Crumbs (2015)*
- *Turbo Kid (2015)*
- *Z for Zachariah (2015)*
- *The End of the World and the Cat's Disappearance (2015)*
- *The Walking Deceased (2015)*
- *Extinction (2015)*
- *Hidden (2015)*
- *Air (2015)*
- *Into the Forest (2015)*
- *JeruZalem (2015)*

- *The Survivalist (2015)*
- *Attack on Titan (2015)*
- *Terminator Genisys (2015)*
- *Maze Runner: The Scorch Trials (2015)*
- *Mad Max: Fury Road (2015)*
- *Maggie (2015)*
- *10 Cloverfield Lane (2016)*
- *Train to Busan (2016)*
- *Seoul Station (2016)*
- *I Am a Hero (2016)*
- *The Fifth Wave (2016)*
- *Cell (2016)*
- *Day of Reckoning (2016)*
- *The Girl with All the Gifts (2016)*
- *Diverge (2016)*
- *The Northlander (2016)*
- *Stephanie (2017)*
- *It Comes at Night (2017)*
- *War for the Planet of the Apes (2017)*
- *Resident Evil: The Final Chapter (2017)*
- *Resident Evil: Vendetta (2017)*
- *Everything Beautiful Is Far Away (2017)*
- *Bokeh (2017)*
- *Blade Runner 2049 (2017)*
- *Cargo (2017)*
- *Here Alone (2017)*
- *Deep (2017)*
- *Bird Box (2018)*

- *Blue World Order (2018)*
- *The Domestics (2018)*
- *Future World (2018)*
- *How It Ends (2018)*
- *I Think We're Alone Now (2018)*
- *In My Room (2018)*
- *Maze Runner: The Death Cure (2018)*
- *Mortal Engines (2018)*
- *The Night Eats the World (2018)*
- *Patient Zero (2018)*
- *A Quiet Place (2018)*
- *Scorched Earth (2018)*
- *What Still Remains (2018)*
- *Blood Quantum (2019)*
- *Zombieland: Double Tap (2019)*
- *The Wandering Earth (2019)*
- *The Silence (2019)*
- *Io (2019)*
- *Terminator: Dark Fate (2019)*
- *Light of My Life (2019)*
- *The Lego Movie 2: The Second Part (2019)*
- *3022 (2019)*
- *2067 (2020)*
- *#Alive (2020)*
- *Alone (2020)*
- *Friend of the World (2020)*
- *Greenland (2020)*
- *Love and Monsters (2020)*

- *Train to Busan Presents: Peninsula (2020)*
- *The Midnight Sky (2020)*
- *Songbird (2020)*
- *How It Ends (2021)*
- *Quarantine (2021)*
- *Silent Night (2021)*
- *Army of the Dead (2021)*
- *Awake (2021)*
- *Don't Look Up (2021)*
- *The Tomorrow War (2021)*
- *Finch (2021)*
- *Mother/Android (2021)*
- *The Mitchells vs. The Machines (2021)*
- *The Matrix Resurrections (2021)*
- *A Quiet Place Part II (2021)*
- *Resident Evil: Welcome to Raccoon City (2021)*
- *Resident Evil: Death Island (2023)*
- *The Wandering Earth 2 (2023)*
- *Bird Box Barcelona (2023)*
- *Zom 100: Bucket List of the Dead (2023)*
- *The Creator (2023)*
- *Leave the World Behind (2023)*
- *Kingdom of the Planet of the Apes (2024)*
- *A Quiet Place: Day One (2024)*
- *Furiosa: A Mad Max Saga (2024)*

Endnotes

1   *By Albert Goodwin - http://www.artrenewal.org/artwork/154/3154/32410/apocalypse-large.jpg, Public Domain, https://commons.wikimedia.org/w/index.php?curid=17090743*

2   *By Stellar Publishing / unidentified staff artist - Wonder Stories, January 1932, Public Domain, https://commons.wikimedia.org/w/index.php?curid=46173326*

3   *By Presumably a work-for-hire for the film's distributor, RKO Radio Pictures. - Scan via Heritage Auctions. Cropped from the original image., Public Domain, https://commons.wikimedia.org/w/index.php?curid=85712019*

4   *By Unknown (propably Universal Pictures) - eBay, Public Domain, https://commons.wikimedia.org/w/index.php?curid=79961661*

5   *Copyrighted by Universal Pictures Co., Inc.. - https://commons.wikimedia.org/wiki/File:The_Birds_original_poster.jpg, Public Domain, https://commons.wikimedia.org/w/index.php?curid=121551687*

6   *By Joseph Pennell - Library of Congress, Prints & Photographs Division, LC-DIG-ppmsca-18343 Public Domain, https://commons.wikimedia.org/w/index.php?curid=4162475*

7   *By anonimous - http://days.pravoslavie.ru/Images/im527.htm, Public Domain, https://commons.wikimedia.org/w/index.php?curid=7065427*

8   *By Walter Reade Organization, Inc. - Night Of The Living Dead (1968) - trailer, Public Domain, https://commons.wikimedia.org/w/index.php?curid=83464005*

9   *By Henry Colburn - https://archive.org/details/lastman01shell, Public Domain, https://commons.wikimedia.org/w/index.php?curid=20230866*

10   *By Lord Byron - The Prisoner of Chillon: https://archive.org/details/prisonerofchillo55byro/page/26/mode/2up, Public Domain, https://commons.wikimedia.org/w/index.php?curid=107438924*

11   *By Matthäus Merian - http://www.johannesoffenbarung.ch/die_himmel/drache_antichrist.php, Public Domain, https://commons.wikimedia.org/w/index.php?curid=13767390*

12   *By Herbert George Wells - https://catalog.hathitrust.org/Record/001693893 via File:The Time Machine (H. G. Wells, William Heinemann, 1895).djvu, Public Domain, https://commons.wikimedia.org/w/index.php?curid=88240392*

13   *By Wings Publishing / Allen Anderson - http://www.philsp.com/mags/sf_tuv.html#two_complete_science_adventure_books, Public Domain, https://commons.wikimedia.org/w/index.php?curid=45588853*

14   *By William Edward Blythe / Stellar Publishing - Science Wonder Stories, June 1929, Public Domain, https://commons.wikimedia.org/w/index.php?curid=43316635*

15   *By H. G. Wells - drzeus.best.vhw.net, Public Domain, https://commons.wikimedia.org/w/index.php?curid=5893115*

16 By Frank R. Paul - https://web.archive.org/web/20070102122025/https://samiz-dat.4t.com/samizdat21/war%20of%20the%20worlds.jpg, Public Domain, https://commons.wikimedia.org/w/index.php?curid=1434642

17 By Henrique Alvim Corrêa - Wells, H.G. War of the Worlds (1906, French ed.), Public Domain, https://commons.wikimedia.org/w/index.php?curid=1567389

18 By Henrique Alvim Corrêa - drzeus.best.vhw.net, Public Domain, https://commons.wikimedia.org/w/index.php?curid=5901070

19 Public Domain, https://en.wikipedia.org/w/index.php?curid=42477134

20 By Henri Lanos - wikia:wiersze:File:'When the Sleeper Wakes' by Henri Lanos 03.jpg ; see also: https://www.flickr.com/photos/57440551@N03/15746774140/in/photostream/, Public Domain, https://commons.wikimedia.org/w/index.php?curid=56155350

21 By Henri Lanos - wikia:wiersze:File:'When the Sleeper Wakes' by Henri Lanos 04.jpg ; see also: https://www.flickr.com/photos/57440551@N03/15746774140/in/photostream/, Public Domain, https://commons.wikimedia.org/w/index.php?curid=56155464

22 By Henri Lanos - wikia:wiersze:File:'When the Sleeper Wakes' by Henri Lanos 06.jpg ; see also: https://www.flickr.com/photos/57440551@N03/15746774140/in/photostream/, Public Domain, https://commons.wikimedia.org/w/index.php?curid=56155480

23 By Henri Lanos - wikia:wiersze:File:'When the Sleeper Wakes' by Henri Lanos 08.jpg ; see also: https://www.flickr.com/photos/57440551@N03/15746774140/in/photostream/, Public Domain, https://commons.wikimedia.org/w/index.php?curid=56155493

24 By Henri Lanos - wikia:wiersze:File:'When the Sleeper Wakes' by Henri Lanos 10.jpg ; see also: https://www.flickr.com/photos/57440551@N03/15746774140/in/photostream/, Public Domain, https://commons.wikimedia.org/w/index.php?curid=56155504

25 By Henri Lanos - wikia:wiersze:File:'When the Sleeper Wakes' by Henri Lanos 14.jpg ; see also: https://www.flickr.com/photos/57440551@N03/15746774140/in/photostream/, Public Domain, https://commons.wikimedia.org/w/index.php?curid=56155532

26 By Experimenter Publishing / Frank R. Paul - http://www.philsp.com/mags/amazing_stories.html, Public Domain, https://commons.wikimedia.org/w/index.php?curid=44986195

27 By Anonymous - Book Scan, Public Domain, https://commons.wikimedia.org/w/index.php?curid=89536776

28 By Ziff-Davis Publishing / Ed Valigursky - http://www.philsp.com/mags/amazing_stories.html, Public Domain, https://commons.wikimedia.org/w/index.php?curid=44352384

29   *By Ziff-Davis Publishing / Ed Valigursky - http://www.philsp.com/mags/amazing_ stories.html, Public Domain, https://commons.wikimedia.org/w/index.php?curid=44352392*

30   *By Signed lower L by Gernsback's illustrator, Frank R. Paul - Retrieved February 18, 2014 from H. Winfield Secor, "An Interview with Nikola Tesla" in Science and Invention", Experimenter Publishing Co., New York, Vol. 9, No. 10, February 1922, p. 912 on Google Books, Public Domain, https://commons.wikimedia.org/w/index.php?curid=31263783*

31   *By Richie Bendall - Own work, CC0, https://commons.wikimedia.org/w/index. php?curid=132270011*

32   *By Ziff-Davis Publishing / Ed Valigursky - http://www.philsp.com/mags/amazing_ stories.html, Public Domain, https://commons.wikimedia.org/w/index.php?curid=44299649*

33   *By Ziff-Davis Publishing / Ed Valigursky - http://www.philsp.com/mags/amazing_ stories.html, Public Domain, https://commons.wikimedia.org/w/index.php?curid=44299645*

34   *By Ziff-Davis Publishing / Norman Saunders - http://www.philsp.com/mags/ amazing_stories.html, Public Domain, https://commons.wikimedia.org/w/index. php?curid=43881578*

35   *By Evelyn De Morgan - Flickr and [1], Public Domain, https://commons.wikimedia.org/w/index.php?curid=658924*

36   *By Julius Schnorr von Carolsfeld - Die Bibel in Bildern, Public Domain, https:// commons.wikimedia.org/w/index.php?curid=5490923*

37   *By Viktor Vasnetsov - http://lj.rossia.org/users/john_petrov/166993.html, Public Domain, https://commons.wikimedia.org/w/index.php?curid=2649874*

38   *By Hans Memling - [1] [2], Public Domain, https://commons.wikimedia.org/w/ index.php?curid=1455943*

39   *By Unknown—the photographer is not credited. Jacket design by Muriel Nasser; published by Random House. - PBA Galleries Auctioneers and Appraisers (direct link to jpg). Cropped to include only the portrait and lightly retouched by uploader., Public Domain, https://commons.wikimedia.org/w/index.php?curid=81250736*

40   *By Jacket design by Muriel Nasser; published by Random House. - Worthpoint (direct link to image). Cropped and lightly retouched by uploader., Public Domain, https://commons.wikimedia.org/w/index.php?curid=81248769*

41   *By Austin Calhoon - http://austincalhoon.com, CC BY-SA 3.0, https://commons. wikimedia.org/w/index.php?curid=26508272*

42   *By Branch of the National Union of Journalists (BNUJ). - https://web.archive. org/web/20080608013945/http://www.netcharles.com/orwell/pics/orwell-union-card.htm, Public Domain, https://commons.wikimedia.org/w/index.php?curid=2001660*

43   *By The National Archives UK - Animal Farm artwork, No restrictions, https:// commons.wikimedia.org/w/index.php?curid=20461423*

44   *By Unknown author - United States Holocaust Memorial Museum, Public Domain, https://commons.wikimedia.org/w/index.php?curid=1253020*

45   *By Alexander Leydenfrost - Scanned from my own collection (Transferred from en.wikipedia to Commons by Hyju.), Public Domain, https://commons.wikimedia.org/w/index.php?curid=17751239*

46   *By unidentified / Greenleaf Publishing - Imagination, 1953 (scan of original magazine), Public Domain, https://commons.wikimedia.org/w/index.php?curid=77847483*

47   *By Ziff-Davis Publishing / unidentified staff artist - Amazing Stories, April-May 1953, Public Domain, https://commons.wikimedia.org/w/index.php?curid=43992543*

48   *By Ziff-Davis Publishing / Barye Phillips - http://www.philsp.com/mags/amazing_stories.html, Public Domain, https://commons.wikimedia.org/w/index.php?curid=43986945*

49   *By Johannes Overbeck and August Mau (1884) - Pompeii in its buildings, antiquities and works of art - Leipzig, 1884, Public Domain, https://commons.wikimedia.org/w/index.php?curid=116774203*

50   *By Jean-Léon Gérôme - phxart.org : Gallery, Pic, Public Domain, https://commons.wikimedia.org/w/index.php?curid=12278*

51   *By Howard Pyle (d. 1911) - https://i.pinimg.com/originals/94/0d/4c/940d4c-06c286a23ac32eeacfe597042e.jpg then enlarged with Topaz Gigapixel AI, Public Domain, https://commons.wikimedia.org/w/index.php?curid=80169126*

52   *By José Moreno Carbonero - Colección, Museo del Prado., Public Domain, https://commons.wikimedia.org/w/index.php?curid=50083271*

53   *By Eric Koch for Anefo - NationaalArchief, CC0, https://commons.wikimedia.org/w/index.php?curid=45225818*

54   *By Rob Mieremet / Anefo - NationaalArchief, CC0, https://commons.wikimedia.org/w/index.php?curid=37443562*

55   *By Anefo - http://proxy.handle.net/10648/abebf8f8-d0b4-102d-bcf8-003048976d84, CC0, https://commons.wikimedia.org/w/index.php?curid=73770363*

56   *By FotograafOnbekend / Anefo - http://proxy.handle.net/10648/abebf588-d0b4-102d-bcf8-003048976d84, CC0, https://commons.wikimedia.org/w/index.php?curid=65833123*

57   *By Fotopersbureau De Boer - FilmopnameGrijpstraen de Gier A'dam, Noord-Hollands Archief, collectieFotopersbureau De Boer, NL-HlmN-HA_1478_17978K00_14, CC0, https://commons.wikimedia.org/w/index.php?curid=119946439*

58   By Nancy WongA - Own work, CC BY-SA 4.0, *https://commons.wikimedia.org/w/index.php?curid=40832961*

59   By Nancy Wong - Own work, CC BY-SA 3.0, *https://commons.wikimedia.org/w/index.php?curid=31294036*

60   By Towpilot - Own work, CC BY-SA 3.0, *https://commons.wikimedia.org/w/index.php?curid=1299960*